Crocheted Gifts
in a Weekend

Crocheted Gifts in a Weekend

70 Quick & Lively Projects to Make

Nola Theiss

Sterling Publishing Co., Inc. New York
A STERLING/LARK BOOK

Editor: Deborah Morgenthal
Design: Chris Bryant
Production: Elaine Thompson
English Translation: Networks, Inc.

Library of Congress Cataloging-in-Publication Data
Theiss, Nola.
    Crocheted gifts in a weekend : 70 quick and lively projects to
make / Nola Theiss.
      p. cm.
    "A Sterling/Lark book."
    Includes index.
    ISBN 0-8069-0970-6
    1. Crocheting--Patterns. 2. Gifts. I. Title.
TT825.T427 1995
746.43'4041--dc20   94-23838
                                CIP

10 9 8 7 6 5 4 3 2

A Sterling/Lark Book

First paperback edition published in 1995 by
Sterling Publishing Company, Inc.
387 Park Avenue South, New York, N.Y. 10016

Produced by Altamont Press, Inc.
50 College Street, Asheville, NC 28801

Photographer, pages 69, 75, 76, 79 and 80, Evan Bracken
All projects and instructions not credited above © Ariadne/Spaarnestad,
Utrecht, Holland
English translation © 1995, Altamont Press

Distributed in Canada by Sterling Publishing
  % Canadian Manda Group, One Atlantic Avenue, Suite 105
  Toronto, Ontario, Canada M6K 3E7

Distributed in Great Britain and Europe by Cassell PLC
  Wellington House, 125 Strand, London WC2R 0BB, England

Distributed in Australia by Capricorn Link (Australia) Pty Ltd.
  P.O. Box 6651, Baulkham Hills, Business Centre, NSW 2153, Australia

Printed and bound in Hong Kong
All rights reserved

Sterling ISBN 0-8069-0970-6 Trade
              0-8069-0971-4 Paper

CONTENTS

Introduction

rabbit pullover
page 90

MENTION THE WORD "CROCHET" and most people instantly get an image of home, mothers and grandmothers, comfortable surroundings, and love. It's no wonder that so many people give and receive crocheted gifts when each gift carries that kind of tradition and meaning. This book contains a collection of traditional and updated gift projects, all in today's fashion colors.

Whether you are an experienced crocheter or a novice, whether you have time for large, complex projects or have to fit in small projects between the demands of your day, we feel certain you will find in this book many projects that meet your level of experience and time requirements. Each project is labelled by difficulty, ranging from easy to experienced. The "Techniques and Notes" and "Glossary of Stitches" sections will explain, with words and illustrations, the basic crochet stitches included in the book. If a special stitch is used in a project, directions for that stitch will accompany the project. When in doubt, find a skilled crocheter to help you; then you will be part of the tradition of passing craft knowledge from one needleworker to another.

The most creative and productive needleworkers know that you should have a few projects in progress at all times—some to carry to meetings, some to work on when you need a challenge, and some to simply relax with while talking with friends. We feel sure that the fruits of your labor—the gifts you create—will be very much appreciated. And if you begin an ambitious project such as a baby blanket, and are not able to finish it for the first grandchild, just hold onto it until the next one comes along!

Babies bring crocheted gifts to mind, and you'll find many adorable projects here that make great shower gifts: a crib blanket, a sweater set, booties, soft toys, and more. There's a terrific nursery ensemble, complete with diaper pin pincushion and bottle warmer. Older children will love the crocheted animals, stuffed with soft fiberfill and lots of love. We've included summer and winter sweaters and tops for toddlers and teens. There's even a matching child's and doll's sweater.

Crochet lends itself beautifully to many aspects of the home. Yes, there are the customary pot holders, but wait until you see them! The designs and colors are both attractive and contemporary. There are probably people on your gift list who'd welcome the European and country touches we've included, such as shelf edgings, jar covers, doilies, and eggcup warmers. For the dining room, you'll find lovely napkin rings and a stunning filet crochet tablecloth.

Pillows with filet crochet edging make a perfect housewarming surprise, as do sachet pillows. On a larger scale, consider making one of the beautiful afghans for a special occasion (or make it for yourself!). Bathroom touches such as soap covers and towels with crocheted edgings make thoughtful presents too.

We've not neglected the outdoors. How about a hammock and matching beach bag? All kinds of mesh bags have become popular these days, and we have provided patterns for a number of varieties, including a backpack and a market bag. For the family that loves to picnic we've included some stunning picnic cushions. And in the winter months, who wouldn't appreciate a crocheted hat or scarf? You'll find scarfs to suit kids, women, and men. (These are so distinctive, you'll want to make one to keep yourself warm.)The designs, stitch techniques, and colors featured in these 70 gift projects are outstanding. You won't have to tell the recipient of your crocheted gift how much you enjoyed making it. Just let them be impressed and grateful!

Nola Theiss

pink petals
page 58

child's hat and scarf
page 78

mohair kittens
page 138

Techniques & notes

the importance of gauge

If there is one absolute in crochet, it is gauge. Getting the correct gauge will ensure that your finished project will be the same size as the original. Make a sample gauge swatch at least four inches (10 cm) square. This has two purposes. First, you will try out the stitch and determine if you feel comfortable doing it and if you like the finished appearance. Secondly, you can measure the gauge and, if necessary, change the hook size in order to get the required number of stitches and rows. In some cases, as with a scarf, it may not be terribly important if a piece is a little larger or a little smaller; in other instances, such as a hat, even the slightest variation in size can be very significant.

Each pattern has a specific gauge—the number of stitches and rows that equal a four-inch (10 cm) square. It is important to crochet a sample square using the yarn and hook size specified before starting the garment. If your square measures less than four inches (10 cm), try a larger hook size. If your square measures larger than four inches (10 cm), try a smaller hook size. Be sure to measure your swatch on a flat surface and avoid stretching it.

reading carefully

When following the instructions, it is very important to read the directions carefully. To the non-crocheter, crochet instructions can appear to be one long run-on sentence, but the careful crocheter will see the significance of a semi-colon as compared to a comma. There's nothing wrong with being creative or adapting a stitch as you work, but an incorrectly placed stitch on one row can cause problems for many rows. On the other hand, sometimes a pattern repeat needs to be entirely worked before you will be able to see if it is correct or not. Don't panic if the pattern looks wrong before all rows are completed. The worst thing that will happen if you make a mistake is that you will have to rip out some stitches or rows. In the end, the yarn will simply be crocheted correctly and no one will ever know. If you think of each new project not only as a finished gift, but also as a learning process for a new stitch, technique, or application, you will not mind (as much!) ripping something out.

hook position

Pay attention to the position of the hook at all times when learning the stitch. Often you will be told to place the hook at the back or front of the work, but remember, unless specified, always insert the hook in the front of the stitch under both loops and work from right to left. These movements will become automatic as you repeat the pattern. Frequently, it will be necessary to skip stitches and then come back to them. Position of the hook is very important in this case as you must know whether to work in front or back of the stitches worked after the skipped stitches.

rounds or rows?

Many of these projects are worked in rounds. Usually rounds are begun by chaining a specified number of stitches, then slip stitching in the first chain to join in a ring. Then you may work stitches in the ring or work stitches in each chain stitch for the first round. Sometimes, the instructions will call for a foundation loop. This is just a big chain stitch. After following the directions for the first round, you will be asked to pull the end of the thread to close the foundation loop so there is no hole at the center.

There are two ways to work in rounds. The first is to slip stitch to join the last stitch of a round to the first stitch of the round, then chain the required number of stitches to form the first stitch. The second method is called the "spiral" method. In this case, do not slip stitch or chain but continue working around. It's a good idea to mark the beginning of the round with a marker or a loop of different colored yarn so you can remember which round you are working on.

When working in rows, begin each row with the appropriate number of chain stitches that will serve as the first sc, dc, etc. of the row. The directions will specify how many chain stitches to make.

asterisks

The asterisk, *, is used in crochet as a repeat sign. All instructions included between two asterisks are to be repeated the total number of times indicated.

increasing

To make a single increase, work two stitches in one stitch. To make a double increase, work three stitches in one stitch. You may want to work in the back loop for one increase and the front loop for the next. To add more stitches at the end of a row, make an additional chain stitch for each additional stitch needed plus the required number of turning chain stitches. On the next row, crochet a pattern stitch in each added chain. Some of the patterns give specific directions for increasing in that pattern stitch. We recommend you follow them or experiment with your own method. The goal is to make as smooth an edge as possible and to get the correct number of stitches.

decreasing

To decrease a single stitch, insert the hook in a stitch, draw through a loop, insert the hook into the next stitch, draw through a loop. Wrap the yarn over the hook; draw the yarn through all three loops.

To decrease two stitches in single or half double crochet, insert the hook in a stitch, draw through a loop, skip the next stitch, insert the hook in the following stitch, draw through a loop. Wrap the yarn over the hook; draw the yarn through all three loops—this is called slip stitching across stitches and is the most common way to decrease at the beginning of a row. To decrease at the end of a row, work across until you have the specified number of stitches unworked at the end of row. Turn and continue as directed across the next row. Be sure to work the correct number of turning chains to beg the following row. To avoid a staircase effect at the edge, you may wish to leave one less stitch unworked than specified, then slip stitch across the first stitch of the following row to give a slanted edge.

yarns and substitutions

When possible, the names of specific yarns have been included in the directions for the project. For the best results, please use those yarns. Always choose a comparable yarn when making a substitution. When it was not possible to name a specific yarn, a description of a type, weight, and yardage has been given to help you choose an appropriate yarn. Changing the style or type of yarn can give significantly different results. Make a swatch if you have any doubt about the finished look. Many of these gifts items will be washed many times. Launder your swatch the way you think the finished gift will be laundered to test the yarn.

tips on using two or more colors

Using the first color, work to the last stitch in one color. Insert the hook in the next stitch, wrap the yarn over the hook, and draw through a loop. Drop the first color to the wrong side of the work and with the second color, wrap the yarn over the hook and draw through a loop. Always work the last wrap over the hook with the new color so that the stitch before the new color is completed with the new color.

Carrying colors across the work—A new color is used to complete the previous stitch before starting the stitch with the changed color. The color not being used is carried across the top of the previous row and the new row is worked over it, making the fabric reversible. Do not draw through the new colored yarn too tightly when using it again or it will distort your work.

Blocks of color—When using two colors alternately across a row, they can be carried along the wrong side of work when not in use as described above. If you are using large blocks or isolated motifs, separate balls or bobbins

are needed for each section. The bobbins or balls of yarn hang at the back of the work. The colors are changed by dropping the first color to the back and using the second color to wrap the yarn over the hook to complete a stitch and start the new stitch with the second color. Either weave the ends in or work over the ends when you change to a new color.

Changing yarns—The directions given above apply to changing yarns as well as changing the color.

hooks

Crochet hooks are made of plastic, coated aluminum, steel, and wood in a range of sizes. The three sizing systems are the U.S. system, the British system, and the metric system. Since all of these patterns were originally worked with metric-size hooks, we are including an interchange chart for metric-U.S.-U.K.-size hooks. If it was possible, we tested the yarn on a U.S.-size hook. However, you may find that there is a slight discrepancy between the chart interchanges and the ones given in the instructions or that another chart in another book is slightly different. There may even be a difference in the same size made by a different manufacturer. In any case, you should use the following chart as a guide only. Always check your gauge and change hooks accordingly.

Steel hooks are generally used with lightweight yarns and threads and for finer, lacy work. Aluminum and plastic hooks are used with most popular weight yarns. Wood hooks are usually found only in the larger and longer lengths. A special hook called an afghan hook is made of

aluminum and has a straight shaft with a knob or cap at one end and a hook at the other. It is used for tunisian stitch in this book. They are sized like the aluminum and plastic hooks.

CROCHET HOOK TRANSLATION TABLE

Metric	U.S.	U.K.
2.5	B/1	12
3	C/2	11
3.25	D/3	10
3.5	E/4	9
4	F/5	8
4.5	G/6	7
5	H/8	6
5.5	I/9	5
6	J/10	4
7	K/10.25	2

finishing techniques

Blocking and pressing—Check the yarn label before proceeding. Always heed the recommendations of the yarn manufacturer. Using the correct measurements, draw an outline of the finished section on heavy paper. Place the paper on a flat surface padded with several soft towels. Using rustproof pins, pin the crocheted piece to the paper. Carefully work the piece to the correct size and shape. Cover the piece with a damp cloth. Following the yarn manufacturer's recommendations, you may either use the steam method or simply weight down the piece.

Steam method: keep the weight of the iron above the work and gently steam the piece. Remove the damp cloth and leave the piece in position to dry thoroughly.

Weight method: place additional towels on top of the damp cloth and then place a wooden board on top of the towels. Leave all in place until the piece is completely dry. Remember any crocheted piece, if allowed to stay wet over a long period of time may lose its color fastness. Be sure to get any excess moisture out of the pieces before blocking.

joining

Pieces of the gifts may be joined together using several methods.

Backstitch—Pin the right sides of the pieces together. Use a yarn or tapestry needle and the yarn used in crocheting the pieces. Work from right to left, using small, even stitches, inserting the needle back through the pieces at the point where it emerged on the previous stitch, bringing the needle through to the front slightly to the left of where it went into the fabric.

Slip stitch—Pin the right sides of the pieces together. Using a crochet hook and yarn, insert the hook through both pieces of the project and draw a loop through the fabric and the loop on the hook. Repeat until the seam is completed.

Invisible weaving (vertical)—Lay the edges to be joined next to one another, right side up. Using a yarn needle and yarn, insert the needle up through the lower half of the end stitch on one piece, draw the thread through. From the front insert the needle through the upper half of the edge stitch on the other piece, draw the yarn through. Continue inserting the needle through alternate sides.

Invisible weaving (horizontal)—This is used on the final row-edges. Lay the edges to be joined next to one another. Using a yarn needle and yarn, insert the needle between the front and the back loops of the edges.

Crochet seams—Hold two pieces with right sides together unless specified otherwise. Insert hook through both thicknesses and draw up loop. Insert hook in next stitch and draw up loop, yo and draw through both loops. Continue until all seams are complete.

terminology

If you are familiar with British crochet terminology, please refer to the following chart of American to British terminology translations.

TERMINOLOGY TRANSLATION TABLE	
AMERICAN TERMS	**BRITISH EQUIVALENTS**
Slip st (sl)	Single crochet (sc)
Single crochet (sc)	Double crochet (dc)
Half double crochet (hdc)	Half treble crochet (htr)
Double crochet (dc)	Treble crochet (tr)
Treble crochet (tr)	Double treble (dtr)
Double treble crochet (dtr)	Treble treble (trtr)

Note: For exact measurements, use centimeters. Conversions to inches from centimeters may cause discrepancies up to 1/4 inch.

$\mathcal{G}$lossary of stitches

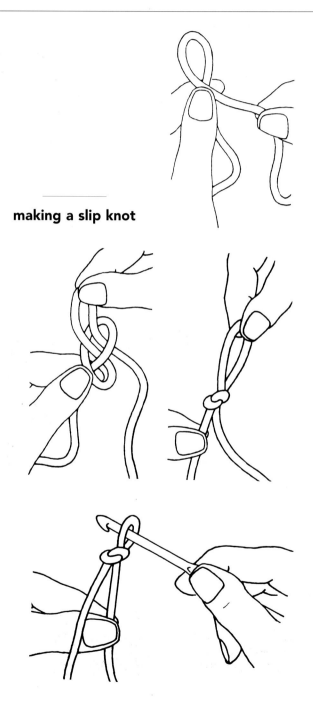

making a slip knot

Many experienced crocheters have never had to work with row-by-row instructions and may find them intimidating. The abundance of abbreviations often makes the instructions appear more complicated than they actually are. The pages that follow explain the stitches and abbreviations used in this book, and a few minutes of study time will pay off when it comes time to begin your first project. (British crocheters should refer to the terminology translation table on page 11.)

yarn over (yo)

Technically a yarn over isn't really a stitch by itself, but no stitch is possible without it. Wrap the yarn around the hook from back to front to form a loop. Depending on the stitch, more yarn overs are formed and drawn through loops and that is, in essence, crochet.

chain stitch (ch)

To start the chain (ch), make a slip knot; insert the hook from right to left through the loop. With the hook in front of the yarn, wrap the yarn around the hook from back to front. With the hook pointing down, draw a new loop through the loop on the hook. This equals one chain stitch.

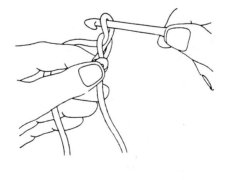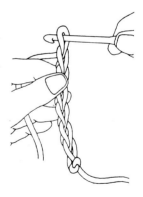

slip stitch (sl stitch)

Insert hook into chain or stitch; wrap the yarn over the hook from back to front; draw a loop through both the chain or stitch and the loop on the hook. This equals one slip stitch.

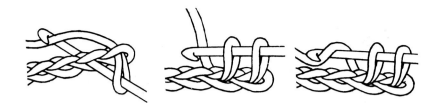

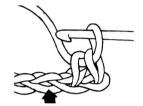

single crochet (sc)

Insert the hook into the second chain from the hook. Wrap the yarn around the hook from back to front. Draw the yarn through the chain, making two loops on the hook. Wrap the yarn around the hook from back to front and draw the yarn through the two loops on the hook. This equals one single crochet stitch. Continue by inserting the hook in the next chain or stitch. After the last stitch, chain 2 and turn; insert the hook into the first stitch to begin the next row.

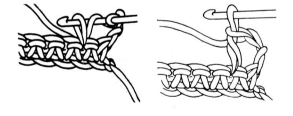

half double crochet (hdc)

Wrap the yarn around the hook from back to front; insert the hook into the third chain from the hook; wrap the yarn over the hook and draw the yarn through the chain, making three loops on the hook. Wrap the yarn around the hook from back to front and draw through the three loops on the hook. This equals one half double crochet stitch. Continue by wrapping the yarn around the hook and inserting the hook in the next stitch. After the last stitch, chain 2 and turn; wrap the yarn over the hook; insert the hook in the first stitch to begin the next row.

double crochet (dc)

Wrap the yarn around the hook from back to front; insert the hook into the fourth chain from the hook; wrap the yarn over the hook and draw the yarn through the chain, making three loops on the hook. Wrap the yarn over the hook and draw it through two loops; wrap the yarn over the hook again and draw the yarn through the last two loops, completing the stitch. Continue by repeating the sequence in each chain stitch. After the last stitch, chain 3 and turn; insert the hook in the second stitch to begin the next row.

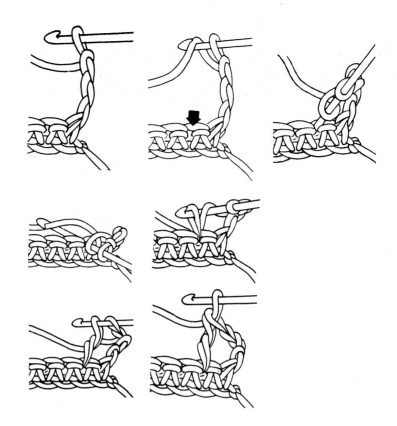

treble crochet (tr)

Wrap the yarn around the hook from back to front twice and insert the hook in the fifth chain from the hook. Wrap the yarn over the hook and draw a loop through the chain, making four loops on the hook. Wrap the yarn over the hook and draw the yarn through two loops; wrap the yarn over the hook and draw the yarn through two more loops; wrap the yarn over the hook again and draw the yarn through the last two loops completing the stitch. Continue by repeating the sequence in each stitch. After the last stitch, chain 4 and turn; insert the hook into the second stitch to begin the next row.

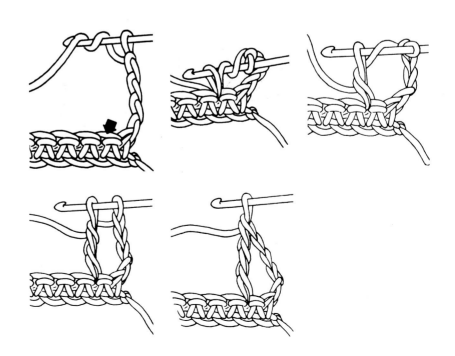

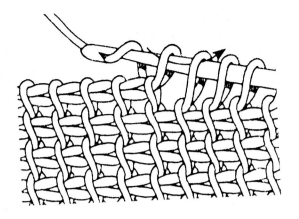

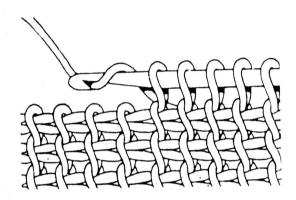

tunisian/afghan stitch

Using an afghan crochet hook, make a chain equal to the desired number of stitches plus 2.

Row 1: Insert the hook into the second chain from the hook, wrap the yarn over the hook and draw a loop through the chain. Continue by wrapping the yarn over the hook and pulling a loop through each chain in the row. Do not turn the work—always work with the right side facing you.

Row 2: The next row is worked by wrapping the yarn over the hook and pulling a loop through the first loop on the hook. Wrap the yarn over the hook and draw a loop through the next two loops on the hook. Repeat until there is one loop left on the hook. The remaining loop forms the first stitch of the next row.

Row 3: Skip the first vertical loop in the row below and insert the hook from right to left through the second vertical loop. Wrap the yarn over the hook and draw the loop through, making two loops on the hook. Continue across the row. Note: insert the hook through the center of the last loop leaving two strands of yarn at the edge.

Row 4: Same as row 2.

Repeat Rows 3 and 4 until desired length is reached.

shrimp stitch

This stitch is used frequently as a finishing edge on necklines and other borders. It is worked like single crochet, but worked in the opposite direction; that is, left to right, instead of right to left. Keep the right side of the work facing you as you work. If shrimp stitch is worked correctly, it will feel as if you are working backwards. If it feels like you are doing single crochet, you have probably turned the work and you *are* doing single crochet.

relief stitches

All relief stitches are the same: basically one inserts the hook around the post, that is the length of the stitch found in a previous row, and works the desired stitch. The texture depends on the stitch, which underlying row is worked, and whether the stitch is worked on the back or front of the work. So they are all similar, but different. We've listed a few variations to give you the general idea.

front relief sc

Work in sc by working around the post of the stitch below. For front relief stitches, insert hook from right to left around the post of the indicated stitch at front of work. Yo, and draw through loop, yo and draw through both loops.

back relief sc

Worked in sc by working around the post of the stitch below. For back relief stitches, insert hook from right to left around the post of the indicated stitch at back of work. Yo, and draw through loop, yo and draw through both loops.

front relief dc

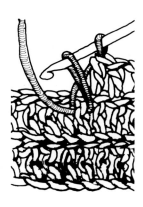

Worked in dc by working around the post of the stitch of the previous row. Yo over hook, insert hook from right to left around the post of the indicated stitch at front of work. Yo, and draw through loop, yo and continue as you would a dc.

back relief dc

Worked in dc by working around the post of the stitch of the previous row. Yo over hook, insert hook from right to left around the post of the indicated stitch at back of work. Yo, and draw through loop, yo and continue as you would a dc.

deep relief stitches

This term refers to the fact that the relief stitch may require you to insert the hook two or more rows below the row you are working on. The only difference between this and the relief stitches above is that the first loop of the stitch will be longer. Otherwise, work normally.

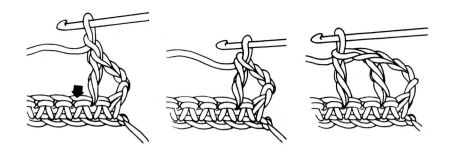

filet stitch

There are many versions of filet stitch, but this is the most common. To make beautiful motifs, fill in the desired squares with one stitch. The last stitch of one square is the first stitch of the following square.

Row 1: *1 dc, ch 2*, rep * to * across.

Row 2 and all following rows: Ch 4 to turn (beg of first square). Always work 1 dc in dc of previous row, chain above chain stitch of previous row.

border stitches

Most American crocheters are not accustomed to the term "border stitch." The first and last stitches, usually the chain at the beginning of the row and the last stitch of the row, are considered border stitches by Europeans because they are worked into the seams and are not part of the pattern. They are worked in the same color as adjoining stitches in most cases. On jacquard patterns, they are usually not included on the chart. When border stitches are used, some explanation will be given in the pattern. Often when joining seams, one sews or crochets between the border stitch and the adjoining stitch.

Some of the sweater patterns use a knitted ribbing rather than a crochet edging. We have included a description of the most commonly used knitted ribbing. If you prefer a crocheted edging, try substituting the post stitch given here.

1/1 ribbing

Row 1: *K1, p1*. Rep * to * across.

Row 2 and all foll rows: Work stitches as established in previous row; that is, knit the stitches that were purled in the previous row and look flat on the 2nd row, and purl the stitches which were knitted in the previous row and have a loop next to the needle.

post stitch ribbing (single crochet)

Worked on an even number of stitches. The idea is always to work a back relief post stitch in a front relief post stitch of the previous row so alternate ridges are formed on the back and front of work.

Row 1: 1 Sc in each ch.

Row 2: Ch 1 (= 1 border stitch) *1 front relief sc, 1 back relief sc*, rep * to *, 1 sc in last space (= 1 border stitch).

Row 3: Ch 1, *1 back relief sc, 1 front relief sc*, rep * to *, 1 sc in last space.

Repeat Rows 2 and 3.

Around the home

Sachet pillow

This lovely pillow is crocheted with care and filled with lavender. Make several using different dried flowers for a sweet-smelling potpourri present.

level

Intermediate

finished measurement

4-1/4 x 4-1/4 in. (11 x 11 cm)

materials

- DMC Cebelia nr. 20 (approx. 405 yds per 50 g skein) 1 skein per pillow in desired color
- Loosely woven fabric for lining
- Fabric for pillow
- 4 pieces of ribbon 10 in. (25 cm) long and 1/8 in. (3 mm) wide
- 25 g of lavender
- Steel crochet hook U.S. size 5 (Metric size .75) or size needed to obtain gauge

To save time, take time to check gauge!

gauge

The crocheted edging is 3-1/4 in. (8 cm) wide. One repeat of pattern is 3/4 in. (2 cm) high.

stitches

Chain (ch), slip st (sl), single crochet (sc), half double crochet (hdc), double crochet (dc), treble crochet (tr)

Note: See pages 8–18 for detailed instructions on stitches and shapings.

directions

With crochet hook, ch 45 + ch 4 = first dc. Row 1: 1 dc in 7th ch from hook, ch 3, skip 3, 1 dc, ch 1, skip 1, 1 dc, ch 1, skip 3 ch, 1 fan = 3 dc, ch 1, and 3 dc in the foll ch, ch 7, skip 9 ch, 1 dc, ch 3, 1 dc, ch 7, skip 9, 1 fan st in the foll ch, ch 1, skip ch 3, 1 dc, ch 1, skip 1 ch, 1 dc, ch 3, skip 3 ch sts, 1 dc, ch 1, skip 1 ch, 1 dc in the last ch. Row 2: Ch 4, 1 dc, ch 3, 1 dc, ch 1, 1 dc, ch 1, 1 fan st in the ch of the underlying fan st, in the center motif: ch 5, 1 dc in the foll dc, *ch 1, 1 dc in the ch-3 arc*, rep * to * 5 times, ch 1, 1 dc in the foll dc, ch 5, rev order of sts to end of row, end with 1 dc in the ch 3 at the beg of the previous row. Row 3: Like row 2, but over the center motif: ch 3, 1 dc and ch 2 in foll 6 dc, 1 dc in the last dc, ch 3. Row 4: Like row 2, but in the center motif: ch 1, 1 dc in the first dc, 1 dc, 1 hdc, 1 sc in the first ch-2 arc, in foll 2 ch 2 arcs: 1 sc, 1 hdc, 1 dc, 1 hdc, 1 sc, ch 3, in the foll 2 ch-2 arcs: 1 sc, 1 hdc, 1 dc, 1 hdc, 1 sc, in the last ch-2 arc: 1 sc, 1 hdc, 1 dc, 1 dc in the last dc, ch 1. Row 5: Like row 2, but over the center motif: ch 7, in the ch-3 arc of the previous row: 1 dc, 1 hdc, 1 sc, ch 7. Rep rows 2 to 5 until piece measures 4 1/4 in. (10.5 cm), end last rep with the 4th row. Foll row: Like row 2, but over the center motif: Ch 9, 1 sc in ch 3 arc, ch 9. Fasten off.

finishing

Block pieces to indicated measurements. Sew the lining and outside of pillow by placing wrong sides tog, sew around, leaving an opening, turn right side out. Stuff the lining with lavender and sew opening closed. Sew the crocheted border around top of the outside pillow. Around the outside edge of crocheted piece, work as foll: join yarn to edge, work 1 sc through the 2 thicknesses of pillow: * ch 3, 1 sc in the 1/8 in. (.5 cm) space of the previous sc*, rep * to *, end with ch 3, sl st in the first st of the round. Thread ribbon through the first and 3rd row of open squares and tack to ends. Tie bows with ends of ribbon. See photo.

$\mathscr{S}$quare pin cushion

Here's a perfect gift for that dedicated embroiderer in your life. You can easily modify the colors to match anyone's taste.

level

Intermediate

finished measurement

4-1/4 in. (11 cm) square

materials

- Mayflower Cotton 8 - Sport weight cotton (186 yds per 50 g skein) 1 skein pink
- Small amount of green pearl cotton
- Piece of fabric 5-1/4 x 10 in. (13 x 25 cm)
- Stuffing
- Crochet hook U.S. size B/1 (Metric size 2) or size needed for size yarn used

stitches

Chain (ch), slip st (sl), single crochet (sc), double crochet (dc)

Note: See pages 8–18 for detailed instructions on stitches and shapings.

directions

With pink, ch 36 = 4-1/4 in. (11 cm). Row 1: Ch 1 = first sc, 1 sc in the 3rd ch from the hook, 1 sc in each of the foll ch. Row 2: Ch 1 = first sc, 35 sc = 36 sc. Always rep the 2nd row until you have 11 rows. Row 12: Ch 1, 10 sc, then 2 sc in green *4 sc in pink, 2 sc in green*, rep * to * once, 11 sc in pink. Work last loop of last st in one color with next color. Row 13: Sc in pink. Row 14: Ch 1, 7 sc in pink, 2 sc in green, *4 sc in pink, 2 sc in green*, rep * to * 3 times, 8 sc in pink. Row 15: Sc in pink. Rep rows 12 to 15, 3 times, end with the 12th row. With pink work 11 rows in sc. Do not fasten off. Let the pink strand hang and work 1 round of green in sc. Round 2: With pink, work 4 dc in each corner with ch 3 counting as first dc, in every dc, ch 1, skip 2 sc, 1 sc in the foll sc, *ch 1, skip 3 or 4 sc (4 dc, ch 1) in the foll sc*, rep * to * 3 times. Along each side there will be 4 waves. Work 1 wave in the corner. Sl st to join at end of round. Work 1 row of shrimp st (like sc, but work left to right instead of right to left). Work in sc in the ch sts of the previous round. Fasten off. Cut a piece of fabric, place crochet piece and fabric right sides tog and sew, leaving an opening to turn right side out. Stuff and close opening.

Soap covers

Slip a pair of scented bath soaps (always a welcome gift) into something very special: their own crocheted covers.

level

Intermediate

finished measurement

Height: 6 in. (15 cm)

materials

- Mercerized crochet cotton nr. 10: 1 skein each colors yellow and turquoise
- Matching ribbon
- Steel crochet hook U.S. size 2 (Metric size 1.5)

stitches

Chain (ch), slip st (sl), single crochet (sc), double crochet (dc)

Note: See pages 8–18 for detailed instructions on stitches and shapings.

directions

Worked in two pieces. Ch 3 = first dc. Ch 31 + ch 4 = first st + ch 1. Row 1: 1 dc in the 7th ch from hook, *ch 1, skip 1 ch, 1 dc in the foll ch*, rep * to * = 15 squares. Row 2: 1 dc, *ch 1, skip 1 ch, 1 dc*, rep * to * 4 times, ch 1, skip ch 1, 1 dc, ch 1 and 1 dc; work 1 fan st in the foll ch = 2 dc, ch 2, 2 dc; ch 2, skip 1 dc, ch 1, 1 dc; 1 fan st in the foll ch, ch 1, skip 1 dc, ch 1, 1 dc and ch 1; 1 dc in foll dc, *ch 1, skip ch 1, 1 dc*, rep * to * 4 times. Row 3: 1 dc, *ch 1, skip 1 ch, 1 dc*, rep * to * 3 times, ch 1, 1 fan st in ch 2 of the fan st, ch 1, then in the ch 2 arc between fan sts: 1 dc, ch 4, 1 dc; ch 1, 1 fan st in ch 2 of fan st, ch 1, 1 dc in 2nd dc after fan st, *ch 1, skip ch 1, 1 dc*, rep * to * 3 times. Row 4: 1 dc, *ch 1, skip 1 ch, 1 dc*, rep * to * twice, ch 1, 1 fan st in ch 2 of fan st, ch 2, 7 dc in ch 4 arc, ch 2, 1 fan st in ch 2 of fan st, ch 1, 1 dc in 2nd dc after fan st, *ch 1, skip ch 1, 1 dc*, rep * to * twice. Row 5: 1 dc, ch 1, skip ch 1, 1 dc, ch 1, 1 fan in ch 2 of fan st, ch 2, work 10 dc on 7 dc, by working 2 dc in every 2nd dc, ch 2, 1 fan in ch 2 of fan st, ch 1, 1 dc on 2nd dc after fan st, ch 1, skip ch 1, 1 dc. Row 6: 1 dc, 1 fan st in 2nd ch of fan st, ch 2, 1 dc in each of the foll 10 dc with ch 1 between them, ch 2, 1 fan st in 2nd ch st of fan st, 1 dc in last dc. Row 7: 1 dc, 1 fan st in ch 2 of fan st, ch 3, skip ch 2 and 1 dc after fan st, *1 sc in ch, ch 3*, rep * to * 9 times, 1 fan st in ch 2 of fan st, 1 dc in last dc. Row 8: 1 dc, 1 fan st in ch 2 of fan st, ch 3, after fan st, skip the ch 3 and 1 sc, *1 sc in ch 3 arc, ch 3*, rep * to * 8 times, 1 fan st in ch 2 of fan st, 1 dc in last dc. Rows 9 to 15: Work same as 8th row, omitting ch 3 arc between fan sts. Row 16: 1 dc, 1 fan st in ch 2 of fan st, ch 3, 1 sc in center ch 3 arc, ch 3, 1 fan st in ch 2 of fan, 1 dc in last dc. Row 17: 1 dc, 1 fan st in 2nd ch of fan st, 1 fan st in ch 2 of foll fan st, 1 dc in last dc. Row 18: 1 dc, 2 dc in ch 2 of fan st, 2 dc in ch 2 of foll fan st, 1 dc in last dc. Fasten off.

finishing

Block pieces to indicated measurements. Along side edges as foll: *2 sc around the outside dc of the row through both thicknesses, 1 picot = ch 4, 1 sc in 4th ch from the hook*, rep * to *, end with 2 sc. Work around the sts of the top edge and end each row with 1 sl st. Row 1: 1 dc, ch 1, skip 1, *in the foll st: 1 dc, ch 1, 1 dc; ch 1, skip 1 ch, 1 dc, ch 1, skip 1 ch*, rep * to *. Row 2: Work 1 dc in each dc with 1 picot between them. Fasten off. Thread ribbon through the 3rd row from the top edge.

Towel edging

Customize a set of towels with an appealing cotton edging. Choose colors that match the gift towels, or trim them in a contrasting color.

level

Intermediate

finished measurement

Width: 1-1/2 in. (4 cm)

Length: 23-1/2 in. (60 cm)

materials

- Mercerized crochet cotton nr. 10: 1 skein color yellow, 1 skein color turquoise
- Crochet hook U.S. size 2 (Metric size 1.75)

stitches

Chain (ch), slip st (sl), single crochet (sc), half double crochet (hdc), treble crochet (tr)

Note: See pages 8–18 for detailed instructions on stitches and shapings.

directions

Picot: ch 4, 1 sc in the 4th ch from the hook. Make a ch 23-1/2 in. (60 cm) long or desired length. Break yarn and leave end hanging. Row 1: Join yarn to the first ch at the beg of the ch and work 1 sc in the first ch, ch 2, skip 3 ch, in the foll st: 1 dc, ch 3, 1 dc; ch 2, skip 3 ch, 1 sc in the foll ch, *1 sc in foll ch, ch 2, skip 3 ch, in the foll st: 1 dc, ch 3, 1 dc; ch 2, skip 3 ch, 1 sc in foll ch*, rep * to * to desired length. Row 2: Ch 4, 7 dc in ch 3 arc, *ch 2, 7 dc in ch 3 arc*, rep * to *, end with 1 tr in first sc of the first row. Row 3: 1 sc in first dc, *ch 3, skip 1 dc, 1 sc in foll dc*, rep * to * 3 times, ch 4, *1 sc in foll dc, **ch 3, skip 1 dc, 1 sc in foll sc**, rep ** to ** *, rep * to *. Row 4: Ch 1, *1 sc in ch 3 arc, ch 3*, rep * to * twice, 1 sc in ch 3 arc, ***ch 5, skip ch 4 arc, **1 sc in ch 3 arc, ch 3**, rep ** to ** twice, 1 sc in ch 3 arc***, rep *** to ***. Row 5: Ch 1, 1 sc in ch 3 arc, ch 1, 1 picot, ch 1, 1 sc in ch 3 arc, *ch 7, 1 sc in ch 3 arc, ch 1, 1 picot, ch 1, 1 sc in ch 3 arc*, rep * to *. Fasten off.

finishing

Along the opposite side of foundation ch, work 1 row of sc as foll: *1 sc in sc, 3 sc in ch 3 arc, 1 picot, 3 sc in ch 3 arc, 1 sc in sc*, rep * to *. Fasten off.

Handkerchief edging

Sure to be a keepsake, this crisp white handkerchief can be masterfully bordered in any color with crochet lacework.

level

Intermediate

finished measurement

4-1/4 in. (11 cm) square

materials

- Crochet cotton of same weight as handkerchief fabric
- Hook size that corresponds to weight of cotton
- Depending on the size of the handkerchief, adjust the number of sts so as to make repeats work evenly.

stitches

Chain (ch), slip st (sl), single crochet (sc), treble crochet (tr)

Note: See pages 8–18 for detailed instructions on stitches and shapings.

directions

Beg at corner of handkerchief. Insert hook in corner, work 1 sc, 3 sc in corner and a row of sc along the edges with 3 sc in each corner. Sl st to join in ring. Round 2: Ch 7, 1 sc in the sc after the corner, * **ch 3, skip 2 sc, 1 sc in the foll sc**, rep ** to ** 3 times, ch 6, skip 5 sc, 1 sc in the foll sc*, rep * to *, then in the foll corner, make 3 ch-3 arcs. For the last corner, ch 7. Sl st to join in ring. Round 3: Work 12 tr in the ch 7 arc of the corner (ch 4 = first tr), *ch 4, 1 sc in the foll ch-3 arc, **ch 3, 1 sc in the foll ch-3 arc**, work ** to ** twice, ch 4, work 8 tr = wave in the ch 6 arc*, rep * to *. In the corner arc, work 12 tr instead of 8 tr. End round with ch 4, 1 sc in the foll ch-3 arc, *ch 3, 1 sc in the foll ch-3 arc*, work * to * 3 times, ch 4, sl st to join in the beg ch 4. Round 4: Ch 3 = first dc**, *ch 1, 1 dc in the foll tr*, rep * to * above the wave, then ch 4, 1 sc in the foll ch-3 arc, ch 3, 1 sc in the foll ch-3 arc, ch 3**, rep ** to **, end with ch 4 instead of ch 3 and sl st in the 3rd ch at the beg. Round 5: Ch 3 = first dc, *ch 2, 1 dc in the foll dc*, rep * to * above the wave st, ch 4, 1 sc in the ch-3 arc, ch 2*, rep * to *, end round with ch 2, sl st in the 3rd ch at the beg. Round 6: 1 sc in the foll ch-2 arc, *ch 4, 1 sc in the 4th ch from the hook, 1 sc in the foll ch-2 arc*, rep * to *, end with 1 sc in the last ch-2 arc of the curve, then ch 3, 1 sc in the first ch-2 arc of the foll wave and rep * to * as above. Sl st to join in round.

Table doily

The variety of stitches in this large doily creates a lace effect that can really dress up a table.

level

Experienced

finished measurement

Each motif has a diameter of 4 in. (10 cm). Work any number of motifs and join into doily.

materials

• Crochet thread nr. 10 (approx. 282 yds per 50 g ball) 1 ball color white

• Steel crochet hook U.S. size 10 (Metric size 1) or size needed to obtain gauge

stitches

Chain (ch), slip st (sl), single crochet (sc), double crochet (dc), treble crochet (tr)

Note: See pages 8–18 for detailed instructions on stitches and shapings.

directions

Ch 13, sl st to join in a ring. End each round with sl st. For first sc, ch 1. For first dc, work ch 3 at beg of round. For first tr, ch 4. Join each round with a sl st near the center of the first arc. Round 1: 24 sc in a ring. Round 2: *1 dc, ch 2, skip 1 sc*, rep * to * 11 times. Round 3: *1 tr in the ch 2 arc, ch 5*, rep * to *. Round 4: *In the ch 5 arc: work 2 tr, 1 picot = ch 4, sl st in the last tr; 1 tr, ch 5*, rep * to * in the foll ch-5 arcs. Round 5: In the middle of the ch 5 arc, *work 1 sc, ch 18, 1 sc in the center of the foll arc, ch 10*, rep * to * = 6 large and 6 small motifs. Round 6: *22 sc in the ch-18 arc, in the ch-10 arc: work 6 sc, 1 picot = ch 4, sl st in the 4th ch from the hook, 6 sc*, rep * to *. Round 7: *In the center 10 sc of the large arc: work 10 tr, ch 16, skip the underlying small arc*, rep * to *. Round 8: *In the group of tr: work 2 sc, ch 4, 3 sc, ch 4 (the joining ch arc), 3 sc, ch 4, 2 sc, in the ch-16 arc: work 4 sc, **3 sc, ch 4**, work ** to ** 3 times in the center ch-4 arc at the beg of the round*. Fasten off. This motif will be the center of the doily.

Second motif: Work same as the first motif until the 7th round. Round 8: Above the group of dc: work 2 sc, ch 4, 3 sc, ch 4, 3 sc,

ch 4, 2 sc, in the ch-16 arc: work 4 sc, ch 4, 4 sc, then ch 2, sl st in the center arc of the center motif, ch 2 and continue in the ch-16 arc of the 2nd motif, then 4 sc, ch 4, 4 sc, finish round like the first motif. Fasten off.

Third motif: Work same as the center motif, joining to the 2nd motif, forming a triangle. Work the same as first motif to the 7th round. Round 8: In the group of tr: work 2 sc, ch 4, 3 sc, ch 4, 3 sc, ch 4, 2 sc, in the ch-16 arc of the 3rd motif, ch 2, 4 sc, ch 4, 4

sc. In the foll group of dc: work 2 sc, ch 4, 3 sc, ch 23, working the first 2 ch sts in the joining arc, ch 21 for the joining arc. Work these ch sts in the center arc of the 2nd motif, turn and ch 10, then join with a sl st in the center of the ch-21 arc. Ch 10 and sl st in the center arc of the center motif. Ch 10 and sl st to the center of the ch-21 arc. Ch 10 and sl st in the first ch of the ch-21 arc. In the center of the triangle, there will be 3 double chains. Work around the 3rd motif, as foll: ch 2, 3 sc,

ch 4, 2 sc in the rem tr, then 4 sc, ch 4, 4 sc and work in the foll arc of the center motif, ch 2, sl st in the center arc of the center motif, ch 2 and continue around. Fasten off. Work in the same manner for each of the motifs, joining to the center motif as above, so all motifs are joined with a double ch 10.

finishing

Block piece to indicated measurements.

it-upons

These roomy, comfortable, and beautiful cushions are a great addition to any activity enjoyed outdoors. (Who says a picnic has to mean "roughing it"?)

level
Intermediate

finished measurement
23 in. (58 cm) x 10-3/4 in. (27 cm); depth: 3-1/4 in. (8.5 cm)

materials
- Mayflower Cotton Helarsgarn - Worsted weight cotton yarn (approx. 86 yds per 50 g skein) 1 skein each color green, yellow, and pink
- Cotton fabric in matching background color, cut 1/4 in. (1 cm) bigger than crocheted piece
- Foam rubber
- Crochet hook U.S. size C/2 (Metric size 3) or size needed to obtain gauge

To save time, take time to check gauge!

gauge
18 sc and 18 rows = 4 in. (10 cm)

stitches

Chain (ch), slip st (sl), single crochet (sc)

Jacquard St: Foll chart in sc. Beg
each row with ch 2. When changing colors, work the last loop of
the last st with the color of the
next st. Use small bobbins of yarn
for each section of color.

*Note: See pages 8–18
for detailed instructions
on stitches and shapings.*

directions

top piece

With background color, ch 27 +
ch 1 to turn. Work the first sc in
the 3rd ch from the hook and
continue in sc foll the chart. Dec
1 st at the right edge of every row
until 1 st remains. Fasten off.

side panels

With background color, ch 14 +
ch 1 to turn. Continue in sc until
piece measures 11-1/2 (9-1/2, 9-
1/2) in.—29 (24, 24) cm. Now for
the yellow (green, pink) cushion,
work as foll: *1 row in yellow
(green, pink), 1 row green (pink,
yellow)*, rep * to * twice, 1 row

in yellow (green, pink), 2 rows in
pink (yellow, green). Continue in
background color for 3-1/2 (8-
1/4, 8-1/4) in.—9 (21, 21 cm)
from the beg. Work in stripe pattern, then continue in background
color until piece measures 55 in.
(138 cm) from beg. Fasten off.

finishing

In background color, work 1 row
in sc around the edges of top.
Join the side panel in a ring. Sew
the fabric to one side of the side
panel and insert foam rubber,
then sew the top piece to the side
panel. See photo.

KEY TO CHART

Green (Pink) Cushion

● = green (pink)

⊠ = yellow (green)

☐ = pink (yellow)

Yellow Cushion

⊠ = yellow

☐ = pink

● = green

yellow triangle ▶

▲ green (pink) triangle

Filet
elegance

Filet crochet bag

This roomy filet crochet bag is a pretty and practical way to tote a crochet or knitting project. Both sides display the distinctive design.

level

Intermediate

finished measurement

14 x 14-1/2 in. (36 x 37 cm)

materials

- Cotton nr. 12 (approx. 285 yds per 50 g skein) 3 skeins color white
- Steel crochet hook U.S. size 2 (Metric size 1.5) or size needed to obtain gauge

To save time, take time to check gauge!

gauge

14 squares and 16 rows = 4 in. (10 cm)

stitches

Chain (ch), slip st (sl), single crochet (sc), double crochet (dc)

Filet stitch: Work by foll chart. Open square = 1 dc, ch 2, skip 2, 1 dc. Filled square = 4 dc. The last dc of the previous square is the first dc of the next square.

Note: See pages 8–18 for detailed instructions on stitches and shapings.

directions

front

Ch 154 + ch 5 = first open square. Row 1: 1 dc in the 9th ch from the hook, *ch 2, skip 2 ch, 1 dc in the foll ch*, rep * to * = 51 open squares. Turn. Row 2: Ch 5, 1 dc in the foll dc = 1 open square, *1 filled square, 1 open square*, rep * to *. Continue by foll chart in open and filled squares. Ch 5 to turn at beg of each row for rows beg with open squares. After the last row of chart, work 4 rows in sc. Work first row as foll: ch 2, 1 sc in the first open square, *3 sc in the foll open square, 2 sc in the foll open square*, rep * to *. Rows 2, 3 and 4: 1 sc in each sc. Ch 1 to turn at beg of each row. Fasten off after the last 4th row. Work the back in the same way.

finishing

Block pieces to indicated measurements. Join the back and front tog by work 4 sc along the edge of the top 4 rows, 2 sc in each square and 5 sc in each corner square. For handles, make 2 chains 13-3/4 in. (35 cm) long and work 4 rows in sc. Fasten off. Sew to top of both pieces.

bag chart

☐ = open square
⊠ = filled square

Row 1

Filet crochet tablecloth

Accent a linen tablecloth by sewing on a filet crochet insert, using handsome openwork stitching along the edges.

level

Intermediate

finished measurement

Insert width: 2-3/4 in. (7 cm) wide
2-3/4 in. (7 cm) = repeat of pat

materials

- Crochet cotton nr. 20 (approx. 405 yds per 50 g skein) 1 ball color white

- Linen 56 in. (140 cm) wide in desired length

- Steel crochet hook U.S. size 4 (Metric size 1) or size needed to obtain gauge

*To save time,
take time to check gauge!*

gauge

18 squares and 20 rows = 4 in. (10 cm)

stitches

Chain (ch), slip st (sl), single crochet (sc), double crochet (dc)

Filet stitch: Work by foll chart. Open square = 1 dc, ch 2, skip 2, 1 dc. Filled square = 4 dc. The last dc of the previous square is the first dc of the next square.

*Note: See pages 8–18
for detailed instructions
on stitches and shapings.*

directions

Ch 40 + ch 3 = first dc. Row 1: 1 dc in the 5th ch from the hook, 1 dc in each of the foll 38 ch. Turn. Row 2: Ch 3, 1 dc in the foll 3 dc = 1 filled square, *ch 2, skip 2 dc, 1 dc in the foll dc*, rep * to * 5 times, *ch 2, skip 2 dc, 1 dc in the foll dc*, rep * to * 5 times, 1 dc in the foll 3 dc. Turn, continue by foll chart in open and filled squares. Ch 3 to turn = first dc. Work to desired length. End with 1 row of dc. Fasten off.

finishing

Block piece to desired measurements. Sew the insert to center of fabric with small stitches, leaving 3/4 in. (2 cm) free at each edge. Make an inner hem 1/4 in. (.75 cm) and a hem 1/2 in. (1.25 cm) along edges. Make openwork hem along edges of filet insert, gathering 2 or 3 strands of linen together by using sketch as a guide.

open work hem stitch ▶

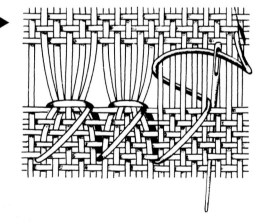

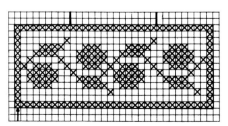

◀ **repeat**

☐ = open square

⊠ = filled square

Row 1

Filet pillows

Striking filet crochet designs adorn this pair of flower trimmed pillows. How nice they'd be for a housewarming!

level

Intermediate

finished measurement

Center (without ruffle): 16 in. (40 cm) diameter

materials

- Crochet cotton #5 - 1 skein white
- Steel crochet hook U.S. size 6 (Metric size 1.75) or size needed to obtain gauge
- Cotton fabric 36 x 18 in. (90 x 45 cm)
- Flowered cotton fabric 16 x 36 in. (40 x 90 cm) for ruffle
- Round pillow forms

To save time, take time to check gauge!

stitches

Chain (ch), slip st (sl), single crochet (sc), half double crochet (hdc), triple (tr)

Note: See pages 8–18 for detailed instructions on stitches and shapings.

Star pillow

directions

End each round with sl st in the top ch at the beg of round. The first ch counts as the first sc, ch 3 counts as the first dc, ch 4 counts as the first tr. Sl st to join each round, then ch as required. Ch 8, join with sl st in a ring. Round 1: Ch 3 = first dc, ch 1, *1 dc in ring, ch 1*, rep * to * 15 times = 16 dc. Round 2: *1 dc in the ch 1 arc, ch 2*, rep * to *. Round 3: *2 dc in the ch 2 arc, ch 2*, rep * to *. Round 4: *2 dc in the ch 2 arc, ch 3*, rep * to *. Round 5: *2 dc, ch 2, 2 dc in the ch 3 arc*, rep * to *. Round 6: *2 dc, ch 2, 2 dc in the ch 2 arc, ch 1, 1 sc between the 2 dc groups, ch 1*, rep * to *. Round 7: *2 dc, ch 2, 2 dc in the ch 2 arc, ch 4*, rep * to *. Round 8: *2 dc, ch 2, 2 dc in the ch 2 arc, ch 3, 1 sc in the underlying sc of the 6th round, 1 sc in the ch 4 arc of the 7th round, work 1 sc, ch 3*, rep * to *. Round 9: *1 dc in the ch 2 arc, ch 11*, rep * to * = 16 arcs. Round 10: *1 dc in the dc, **ch 1, 1 dc**, rep ** to ** 5 times in the 11 ch arc. Work in dc in the ch sts, instead of skipping the ch sts *, rep * to * = 96 dc. Round 11: *1 dc in the foll ch, ch 1, 1 dc in the foll ch, ch 2*, rep * to *. Round 12: *1 dc in the foll ch arc, ch 2*, rep * to *. Rounds 13 and 14: Like round 12. Round 15: *1 dc in the foll ch arc, ch 3, 1 dc in the foll ch arc, ch 2, 1 dc in the foll ch arc, ch 2*, rep * to *. Round 16: *3 dc in the foll ch 3 arc, ch 8, skip 2 ch 2 arcs, rep * to * = 32 arcs. Round 17: *2 dc, ch 2, 2 dc in the center of the ch 8 arc, ch 6*, rep * to *. Round 18: *2 dc, ch 2, 2 dc in the ch 2 arc = fan, ch 2, 1 sc in the ch 6 arc, ch 2*, rep * to *. Round 19: *1 fan in the ch 2 of the fan, ch 3, 1 sc in the sc, ch 3*, rep * to *. Round 20: *1 fan in the fan, ch 4, 1 sc in the sc, ch 4*, rep * to *. Round 21: *1 fan in the fan, ch 5, 1 sc in the sc, ch 5*, rep * to *. Fasten off.

finishing

Block pieces to indicated measurements. Cut a paper circle with a diameter of 16 in. (40 cm) with 1/4 in. (1 cm) seam allowance. Cut out a circle of fabric. Cut paper pattern in half and cut out two pieces of fabric, allowing a 1/4 in. (1 cm) seam allowance along straight edge. Fold straight edge seam allowance to inside and sew in place. Lay the crocheted piece over the right side of fabric circle and baste around edges. Cut flowered fabric in 4-3/4-in. - wide (12 cm) strips 100 in. (2.50 m) long. Sew ends of strips to form a ring. Fold the fabric in half, wrong sides together. Gather the open edges and fit around right side of crocheted fabric and pin in place. Place the half circles right sides together with other piece and sew around, leaving an opening. Turn right side out. Stuff with form and sew back seam together.

Pillow with six leaves

directions

Ch 6 and sl st to join in a ring. Round 1: Ch 3 = 1 dc, ch 3, *1 dc in the ring, ch 3*, rep * to * 4 times = 6 dc. Round 2: *4 dc in the ch 3 arc, ch 3*, rep * to *. Round 3: 1 sc in the last ch of the previous round, *ch 5, 1 sc, ch 6, 1 sc in the foll ch 3 arc*, rep * to *. On the last rep, work the last sc to the last sc, end round with 1 sl st in first sc of the round = 12 arcs. Round 4: *4 dc in the ch 5 arc, ch 2, 1 dc, ch 3, 1 dc, ch 2 in the ch 6 arc*, rep * to * 5 times. Round 5: Sl st in the first ch 3 arc, *1 dc, ch 1, 1 dc, ch 1, 1 dc in the ch 3 arc, ch 10*, rep * to *. Round 6: *1 dc in ch 1 arc, ch 1, 1 dc in the center dc, ch 1, 1 dc in the foll ch 1 arc, ch 2, 11 dc in the ch 10 arc, ch 2*, rep * to *. Round 7: *1 dc in the foll ch 1 arc, ch 1, 1 dc in the foll ch 1 arc, ch 1, 1 dc in the ch 2 arc, ch 2, 9 dc in the center 9 dc of the group of 11 dc, working in the back loop, ch 2, 1 dc in the ch 2 arc, ch 1*, rep * to *. Round 8: * **1 dc in the ch 1 arc, ch 2**, rep ** to ** twice, 1 dc in the ch 2 arc, ch 2, 7 dc in the center 7 dc of the group of 9 dc, worked in the back loops, ch 2, 1 dc in the ch 2 arc, ch 2, 1 dc in the ch 1 arc, ch 2*, rep * to *. Round 9: **1 dc in the ch 2 arc, *ch 2, 1 dc in the ch 2 arc*, rep * to * twice, ch 3, 5 dc in the center 5 dc of the group of 7 dc, ch 3*, **1 dc in ch 2 arc, ch 2***, rep *** to *** 3 times**, rep ** to **. Round 10: ** *1 dc in the ch 2 arc, ch 3*, rep * to *, 1 dc in the ch 3 arc, ch 3, 3 dc in the center 3 dc of the group of 5 dc worked in back loops, ch 3, 1 dc in the ch 3 arc, ch 3, *1 dc in the ch 2 arc, ch 3*, rep * to * 3 times **, rep ** to ** = 48 arcs of ch 3. Round 11: ** *1 tr in the ch 3 arc, ch 3*, rep * to * 3 times, 1 tr in the center dc of the group of 3 dc, ch 3, *1 tr in the ch 3 arc, ch 3*, rep * to * 5 times **, rep ** to ** = 54 tr with ch 3 between. Round 12: *4 tr in the ch 3 arc, ch 1*, rep * to *. Round 13: *1 sc in the ch 1 arc, ch 7*, rep * to * = 54 arcs. Round 14: *1 sc in the center of ch 7 arcs, ch 7*, rep * to *. Round 15: *1 sc in the center of ch 7 arc, ch 5*, rep * to *. Round 16: *5 dc in the ch 5 arc, ch 1*, rep * to *. Round 17: *1 sc in the ch 1 arc, ch 8*, rep * to *. Round 18: *1 sc in the center ch 8 arc, ch 8*, rep * to *. Round 19: *1 sc in the center ch 8 arc, ch 6*, rep * to *. Round 20: *6 dc in the ch 6 arc, ch 1*, rep * to *. Round 21: *1 sc in the ch 1 arc, ch 8*, rep * to *. Fasten off.

finishing

Work same as star motif pillow.

Kitchen classics

Egg warmers

With their chic hats and ruffled coats, these little people bring a festive touch to the table (and keep the eggs warm!). One basic design is used; the colors and details make each an individual.

level
Intermediate

finished measurement
3-1/2 in. (9 cm) high, 6-1/2 in. (17 cm) wide

materials
- Mercerized cotton nr. 10 (approx. 230 yds per 50 g skein) in assorted colors
- Steel Crochet hook U.S. size 6 (Metric size 1.75) or size needed to obtain gauge
- Plastic balls 1-1/4 in. (3 cm) in diameter

    To save time, take time to check gauge!

gauge
15 sc and 17 rows = 2 in. (5 cm)

stitches
Chain (ch), slip st (sl), single crochet (sc), double crochet (dc)

Note: See pages 8–18 for detailed instructions on stitches and shapings.

egg warmer

The egg warmers are all made the same, with different accessories. Beg with ch 2 = first sc and ch 3 = first dc of the round. Sl st to join in round to first st. Picot = ch 3, 1 sc in the first ch. Use whatever color desired.

head

Make a loop and work 10 sc in loop, then draw thread tightly to close loop. Round 2: Sc, working 2 sc in every 2nd st = 15 sc. Round 3: Sc, working 2 sc in every 3rd st = 20 sc. Round 4: Sc, working 2 sc in every 4th st = 25 sc. Round 5: 25 sc. Round 6: Sc, working 2 sc in every 5th st = 30 sc. Rounds 7 - 10: 30 sc. Round 11: Sc, working every 5th and 6th st tog = 25 sc. Round 12: Sc, insert plastic ball and crochet around it. Round 13: Sc, working every 4th and 5th st tog = 20 sc. Round 14: Sc, working every 3rd and 4th st tog = 15 sc. Round 15: Sc, working every 2nd and 3rd st tog = 10 sc. Cut thread, leaving a 4 in. (10 cm) tail. Thread through sts, gather tightly, and tack to head to use later for the skirt.

skirt

Make a loop and work 10 sc in loop. Draw thread tightly to close loop. Round 2: Sc, working 2 sc in every st = 20 sc. Round 3: 20 sc. Round 4: Sc, working 2 sc in every 2nd st = 30 sc. Rounds 5 and 6: 30 sc. Round 7: Sc, working 2 sc in every 3rd st = 40 sc. Rounds 8, 9, and 10: 40 sc. Round 11: Sc, working 2 sc in every 4th st = 50 sc. Rounds 12–19: 50 sc. Round 20: 50 shrimp st (work in sc, working left to right instead of right to left). Fasten off.

collar

Ch 15 + ch 2 = first sc. Round 1: Sc in 4th ch from hook and in each ch across = 15 sc. Round 2: *Ch 3, skip 1 sc, sc in next sc*, rep * to * 6 times = 7 arcs. Round 3: In each arc: 2 dc, 1 picot, 2 dc and 1 picot. Cut thread 8 in. (20 cm) long. Fasten off.

buttons

Ch 10 in a loop. Draw thread tightly to close loop. Thread through loops of sts to form a ball. Sew 2 buttons on to skirt.

ears

Ch 10 in a loop. Draw thread tightly to close loop. Fold the circle double and sew outside edges to each other. Sew to head.

eyes, nose, mouth, hair, and eyebrows

Embroider in stem or satin st. Use photo as a guide.

hats

Hat 1: Round 1: Work 10 sc in loop. Round 2: Sc, work 2 sc in each sc = 20 sc. Round 3: Sc, work 2 sc in every 2nd sc = 30 sc. Round 4: Sc, work 2 sc in every 15th sc = 32 sc. Rounds 5 - 8: 32 sc. Round 9: 32 sc. Round 10: *Ch 3, skip 1 sc, 1 sc in the foll sc*, rep * to * 14 times, end with ch 3, sl 1 in the first st. Round 11: In every arc: 2 sc, 1 picot and 2 sc.

Hat 2: Round 1: Work 12 sc in a loop. Round 2: *Ch 5, skip 1 sc, 1 sc in 1 sc*, rep * to * = 6 loops. Round 3: Work 7 sc in every arc. Round 4: *Ch 5, 1 sc in the 4th sc, ch 5, 1 sc between the 2 loops*, rep * to * - 12 loops. Rounds 5–8: Join with a sl st at the center of the arc, *ch 5, 1 sc in the foll arc*, rep * to *. Round 9: Like round 5, but work ch 3 instead of ch 5. Round 10: In every arc: 3 sc = 36 sc. Round 11: 1 sc in every sc.

Hat 3: Ch 36 + ch 2 = first sc. Work back and forth in rows. Row 1: Work 1 sc in each ch, beg with 4th ch from hook = 36 sc. Rows 2 and 3: 36 sc. Row 4: Sc, work every 7th and 8th sc tog = 32 sc. Row 5: 32 sc. Row 6: Sc, work every 6th and 7th sc tog = 28 sc. Row 7: 28 sc. Row 8: Sc, work every 5th and 6th sc tog = 24 sc. Row 9: 24 sc. Row 10: Sc, work every 4th and 5th sc tog = 20 sc. Row 11: 20 sc. Row 12: Sc, work every 3rd and 4th sc tog = 16 sc. Row 13: 16 sc. Row 14: Sc, work every 2nd and 3rd sc tog = 12 sc. Fasten off. Cut the thread. Around the foundation row work 2 rounds as foll: Round 1: 1 sc in each sc = 36 sc. Round 2: 36 sc. Make a button and sew to point.

Hat 4: For the upper edge, work rounds 1 to 4 same as skirt = 30 sc. Round 5: Sc, work 2 sc in every 5th sc = 36 sc. Fasten off. For the border, work ch 36 + ch 2 in the first sc. Round 1: 1 sc in every ch, beg with 4th ch from hook = 36 sc. Rounds 2–4: 36 sc. Round 5: 36 sc, work this round of the center piece and the border tog through both thicknesses. Fasten off.

Hat 5: Work rounds 1 to 8 same as skirt (8th round = 40 sc). Round 9: Sc, work 2 sc in every 4th sc = 50 sc. Rounds 10, 11, and 12: 50 sc. Round 13: 50 shrimp st.

Hat 6: Work rounds 1 to 6 same as skirt (6th round = 30 sc). Round 7: Sc, work 2 sc in each 10th sc = 33 sc. Rounds 8–14: 33 sc. Rounds 15 to 16: 33 sc. Fasten off. Make a pleat on each side of point.

Napkin rings

A set of these elegant snowflake-white napkin rings would make a much appreciated housewarming gift.

level

Intermediate

materials

- Crochet cotton 1 skein color white
- Plastic ring: 1-1/4 in. (3.5 cm) in diameter
- Crochet hook U.S. size B/1 (Metric size 2)

stitches

Chain (ch), slip st (sl), single crochet (sc), double crochet (dc), treble crochet (tr)

Note: See pages 8–18 for detailed instructions on stitches and shapings.

directions

Work in sc, working tight sts around ring. Round 1: *Skip 2 sts, in the foll st: 1 dc, 1 picot: ch 3, 1 sc in the 3rd ch from the hook, 1 tr, 1 picot, 1 tr, 1 picot, 1 dc, skip 2 sts, 1 sc in the foll st*, rep * to * 4 times or as many times as required to work 3/4ths of the way around ring. Fasten off.

ar cover

Dress up a jar of jam with this lovely cover, and present it to a friend with a sweet tooth and a discerning eye for beauty.

level

Intermediate

finished measurement

Diameter 6-1/4 in. (16 cm)

materials

- Crochet thread nr. 10 (approx. 282 yds per 50 g ball) 1 ball color white
- Ribbon
- Steel crochet hook U.S. size 10 (Metric size 1) or size needed to obtain gauge

stitches

Chain (ch), slip st (sl), single crochet (sc), double crochet (dc), treble crochet (tr)

Note: See pages 8–18 for detailed instructions on stitches and shapings.

directions

Ch 13, sl st to join in a ring. End each round with 1 sl st, for the first sc, ch 1. For each first dc, work ch 3 at beg of round. For each first tr, ch 4. Join each round with a sl st near the center of the first arc. Round 1: 24 sc in a ring. Round 2: *1 dc, ch 2, skip 1 sc*, rep * to * 11 times. Round 3: *1 tr in the ch-2 arc, ch 5*, rep * to *. Round 4: *In the ch-5 arc: work 2 tr, 1 picot = ch 4, sl st in the last tr; 1 tr, ch 5*, rep * to * in the foll ch-5 arcs. Round 5: In the middle of the ch-5 arc, *work 1 sc, ch 18, 1 sc in the center of the foll arc, ch 10*, rep * to * = 6 large and 6 small motifs. Round 6: *Work 22 sc in the ch-18 arc, work in the ch-10 arc: work 6 sc, 1 picot = ch 4, sl st in the 4th ch from the hook, 6 sc*, rep * to *. Round 7: *In the center 10 sc of the large arc: work 10 tr, ch 16, skip the underlying small arc*, rep * to *. Round 8: *In the group of tr: work 2 sc, ch 4, 3 sc, ch 4, 3 sc, ch 4, 2 sc, in the ch-16 arc: work 1 sc, ch 4, **3 sc, ch 4**, work ** to ** 6 times, 1 sc*, rep * to * = 60 ch-4 arcs. Round 9: *1 sc in the ch-4 arc, ch 3*, rep * to *. Round 10: *1 tr in the ch-3 arc, ch 3*, rep * to *. Rounds 11 and 12: *1 sc in the ch-3 arc, ch 5*, rep * to *. Round 13: In each ch-5 arc: *work 2 dc, 1 picot as on round 4, 1 tr, ch 3,* rep * to *. Fasten off.

finishing

Block piece to indicated measurements. Thread ribbon between the 8th and 9th rounds.

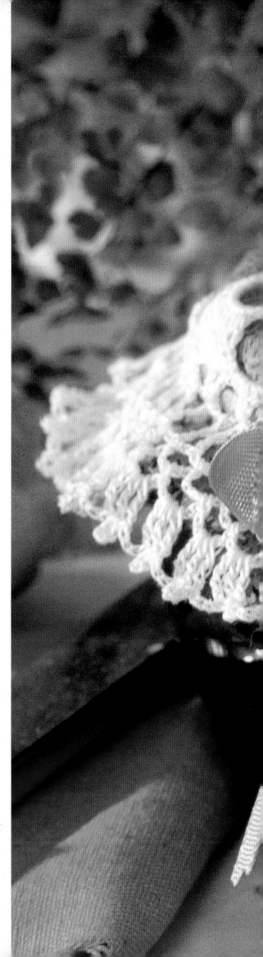

ink doily

This pin-wheel pattern doily adds elegance to any place setting. Make several in pink, or choose different colors to match a particular decor.

level

Experienced

finished measurements

9-1/2 in. (24 cm) in diameter

materials

- Crochet cotton Nr. 6 one skein color white
- Steel crochet hook U.S. size 9 (Metric size 1) or size needed to obtain gauge

stitches

Chain (ch), slip st (sl), single crochet (sc), half double crochet (hdc)

Note: See "Stitches and Techniques" for detailed instructions on stitches and shapings.

doily

Ch 7, sl st to join in ring. Work in rounds, do not sl st to join at end of round unless otherwise indicated. Round 1: Work 16 sc in ring. Round 2: *Ch 3, skip 1 sc, 1 sc*, rep * to * 7 times = 8 ch-3 arcs. Round 3: *3 sc in the ch-3 arc, ch 2*, rep * to * 7 times. Round 4: *Skip 1 sc, 2 sc, 2 sc in the ch-2 arc, ch 2*, rep * to * 7 times. Round 5: *Skip 1 sc, 3 sc, 2 sc in the ch-2 arc, ch 2*, rep * to * 7 times. Round 6: *Skip 1 sc, 4 sc, 2 sc in the ch-2 arc, ch 2*, rep * to * 7 times. Round 7: *Skip 1 sc, 5 sc, 2 sc in the ch-2 arc, ch 2*, rep * to * 7 times. Round 8: *Skip 1 sc, 6 sc, 2 sc in the ch-2 arc, ch 2*, rep * to * 7 times. Round 9: *Skip 1 sc, 7 sc, ch 2, 1 sc in the ch-2 arc, ch 2*, rep * to * 7 times. Round 10: *Skip 1 sc, 5 sc, ch 2, 1 sc in the ch-2 arc, ch 2, 1 sc in the foll ch-2 arc, ch 2*, rep * to * 7 times. Round 11: *Skip 1 sc, 13 sc, ch 2, 1 sc in the ch-2 arc, ch 2, 1 sc in the foll ch-2 arc, ch 2, 1 sc in the foll ch-2 arc, ch 2, 1 sc in the foll ch-2 arc, ch 2*, rep * to * 7 times. Round 12: *Skip 1 sc, 1 sc in each of the foll sc, ch 3, 1 sc in the foll ch-2 arc, **ch 2, 1 sc in the foll ch-2 arc**, rep ** to ** 3 times, ch 2*, rep * to *. Round 13: *Work 13 dc in the ch-3 arc, 1 sc in the foll ch-2 arc, **ch 2, 1 sc in the foll ch-2 arc**, rep ** to ** 3 times*, rep * to * 7 times = 8 fan sts of 13 sts with ch-2 arcs between them. Round 14: *Ch 3, 1 sc in the 4th dc of the fan st, ch 3, 1 sc in the 9th dc of the fan st, ch 3, 1 sc in the foll ch-2 arc, ch 3, 1 sc in the foll ch-2 arc, ch 3, 1 sc in the foll ch-2 arc*, rep * to * 7 times = 40 arcs of ch 4. Round 15: Sl over the foll ch-3 arc, ch 3 = first dc, ch 1 and 1 dc in the same arc, ch 1, *work in the foll ch-3 arc: 1 dc, ch 1, 1 dc and ch 1*, rep * to *. Sl st to join in the 3rd ch = 80 dc with 1 ch st after each dc. Round 16: *1 dc in the foll arc, ch 1*, rep * to *. Sl st to join in round. Round 17: Alternate 2 and 3 dc around each ch arc = 200 dc. Sl st to join in round. Round 18: Work 3 groups of 3 dc worked tog with ch 1 between them. Ch 3 = first dc, yo, draw through loop in foll st, yo, draw through 2 loops, yo, draw through loop in foll st, yo, draw through 2 loops, yo, draw through 2 loops, ch 1, *yo, draw through loop in foll st, yo, draw through 2 loops, yo, draw through loop in foll st, yo, draw through 2 loops = 4 loops on hook, yo, draw through 3 loops, draw through 2 loops, ch 1*, rep * to *. Dec 10 sts in this round by working 3 dcs worked tog = 70 dcs worked tog. Sl st to join in round. Now continue in rounds without joining. Round 19: *Ch 2, 1 sc in the foll ch arc*, rep * to *. Round 20: Like round 19. Sl st to join in round. Break yarn.

border

Ch 3. Sl st to join in ring. Round 1: Ch 5 = turning ch, work 1 dc, ch 2 and 1 dc in ring. Turn. Round 2: Ch 5 = turning ch, work 1 dc, ch 2 and 1 dc in ch-2 arc, turn. Rep the 2nd round 6 times. After the last repeat do not turn = bias band. For the curve at the left, in the turning chain, ch 2, *1 dc, ch 1*, rep * to * 7 times and end after the last dc, ch 2, 1 sc in the foll turning ch. Turn, ch 2, *4 dc in each of the foll ch-2 arc, 3 dc in the foll arc, 4 dc in the foll arc*, rep * to * twice = 30 dc. Now

work in the sts of the bias band: 1 dc, ch 2 and 1 dc in the ch-2 arc. Turn, ch 5, 1 dc, ch 2 and 1 dc in the ch-2 arc of the border, above the 30 dc of the curve, work *ch 2, 1 dc*, rep * to * 13 times, work the first dc in the 2nd dc of the group, skip 1 dc after the dc and in the middle of the curve, skip 2 dc 4 times. After the last dc, ch 2, 1 sc in turning ch. Turn, ch 2, in each ch arc: 3 dc = 3 dc in the curve, then ch 1 and 1 dc, ch 1, 1 dc in the ch-2 arc of the bias band. Work round 2, 9 times in the bias band and rep from for the foll curves. Work 10 curves and end with the last row of the curve = 3 dcs 14 times. Ch 5 to turn and work 1 dc, ch 2 and 1 dc in the ch-2 arc of the bias band = 60 turning ch of the bias band.

Along the outside edges of the 10 curves, work: ch 2, 1 hdc in the 2nd dc, *ch 2, 1 hdc*, rep * to * 18 times, skip 2 sts twice, **skip 1 dc once, skip 2 dc twice**, rep ** to ** 14 times, end with ch 2 and 1 sc in the turning ch after the curve*, rep from along the foll curves. Turn and work picot row: *1 dc in the ch arc, ch 3 and 1 sc in the post of the last dc*, rep * to * to end of curve, work before and after the sc of the turning ch, 1 sc = 1 picot. Sl st to join in round. Break yarn. Now work around the center piece. Fasten yarn in the first ch arc of the last round of the center piece and work in the arc: ch 1, ch 2, sl st in the first turning ch of the border, ch 2, 1 sc in the foll ch arc of the center piece and sl st to join in the first sc. Fasten off. Block piece to indicated measurement.

Pot holders

These fantastic contemporary pot holders take the cliche out of giving a pot holder as a gift. The colors and designs are fresh and vibrant. There's a friendly fish, two stunning floral designs, a bold study in contrasting colors, and a childlike drawing of home sweet home. You're sure to find a motif that will make a much appreciated present.

Home sweet home

level
Intermediate

finished measurement
6-3/4 x 7 in. (17 x 18 cm)

materials
- Mayflower Cotton 8- Sport weight yarn (approx. 186 yds per 50 g skein) 1 skein each color blue, light green, green, yellow, white, red, orange, and rose
- Crochet hook U.S. size C/2 (Metric size 2.5) or size needed to obtain gauge

*To save time,
take time to check gauge!*

gauge
21 sc and 24 rows = 4 in. (10 cm)

stitches
Chain (ch), slip st (sl), single crochet (sc), double crochet (dc)

Deep Deep relief dc: Work the dc on the right side around the post of the previous row as foll: yo, insert hook from front to back through the underlying st of the previous row, coming through front at the left so that the post is worked. Draw through a long loop and make a dc in the normal manner, but with longer loops than a normal dc.

Note: See pages 8–18 for detailed instructions on stitches and shapings.

pot holder
With green, ch 33 + ch 1 = first st. Row 1: Sc in 3rd ch from hook and in each ch across = 33 sc. Row 2: Ch 3 = first dc, dc in sc across = 33 dc. End with 1 dc in the ch at the beg of the first row. Work the last loop of the last st with light green. Row 3: With light green, ch 1 to turn, 1 sc in the last dc 2 rows below, *1 deep deep relief dc around the foll underlying sc 2 rows below= row 1, 1 sc in the foll dc, then a dc under the skipped deep deep relief dc*, rep * to *, work the last sc in the 3rd ch from the beginning dc. Row 4: Ch 3 = first dc, *1 dc in the foll deep deep relief dc, 1 dc in the foll sc*, rep * to * to last dc in the last sc and make the last loop in green. Row 5: With green, ch 1 to turn, 1 sc in the last worked dc

of the previous row, *1 deep deep relief dc around the underlying deep deep relief dc 2 rows below, 1 sc in the foll dc*, rep * to *, work the last sc in the 3rd ch of the first dc. Rep rows 2 to 5 for a total of 13 rows. The last row is a right side row. Work the last loop in blue. Row 14: With blue on the wrong side of the work, ch 1 to turn, 1 sc in each st = 33 sc. Rep the 14th row until piece measures 6-3/4 in. (17 cm). Work 3 rounds around the potholder as foll: Round 1: With green on green sections and blue on blue sections, work 1 sc in each sc in each row, working through both loops of underlying st. In the corner st: 1 sc, ch 1 and 1 sc, sl st in first st to join. Fasten off. Round 2: Join yellow yarn in the upper left corner, 1 sc, ch 18 and 1 sc in the ch at

the corner, 1 sc in each sc, in the next and all foll corner sts: 1 sc, ch 1, 1 sc, sl st to join. Round 3: Ch 1, 1 sc in each st of ch 18 and continue same as round 2. Sl st to join. Fasten off.

house

With white, ch 9 + ch 1 to turn. Row 1: 1 sc in the 3rd ch from the hook, 1 sc in each of the foll ch = 9 sc. Row 2: Sc, working 2 sc in the last sc = 10 sc. Row 3: Sc, working 2 sc in the first sc = 11 sc. Row 4: Like row 2. Row 5: Like row 3. Row 6: Like row 2 = 14 sc. Row 7: Sc, working the first 2 sc tog = 13 sc. Row 8: Sc, working the last 2 sc tog = 12 sc. Row 9: Like row 7. Row 10: Like row 8. Row 11: Like row 7 = 9 sc. Fasten off.

roof

With red, work 2 rows of sc along the slanted edges of house. Row 1: 2 sc in the first row, 1 sc in the 2nd to the 5th rows, 3 sc in the 6th row, 1 sc in the 7th to 10th rows and 2 sc in the 11th row = 15 sc. Row 2: Sc: 2 sc in the first and last sc and 3 sc in the center sc at the point = 19 sc. Fasten off.

trunk

With yellow, ch 5 + ch 1 to turn. Row 1: 1 sc in the 3rd ch from the hook, 1 sc in each of the foll ch = 5 sc. Row 2: 5 sc. Fasten off. Leaves: Row 1: Make a loop with green and work 6 sc in loop. Work in rounds without sl stitching to join at end of round. Round 2: 2 sc in each sc = 12 sc. Round 3: 2 sc in every 2nd sc = 18 sc. Round 4: 2 sc in every 3rd sc = 24 sc, sl st to join. Fasten off.

sun

With yellow, work same as first 3 rounds of leaves. Sl st to join and fasten off.

finishing

Use satin stitch to embroider windows and door using the photo as a guide. With stem stitch, outline window panes as shown in photo. Embroider apples and flowers and birds in chain st. Embroider centers of flowers with 2 satin stitches. Sew on houses, trees and sun.

*E*mbroidered flowers & gold set

level
Intermediate

finished measurement
Flower pot holder: 7 x 7 in. (18 x 18 cm)

Gold pot holder: 7-1/2 x 7-1/2 in. (19 x 19 cm)

materials
- Mayflower Cotton 8 - Sport weight yarn (approx. 186 yds per 50 g skein)
- *Flower pot holder:* 1 skein each color light yellow, light green, white, and desired colors for embroidery
- *Gold pot holder:* 1 skein color gold
- Crochet hook U.S. size B/1 (Metric size 2.5) or size needed to obtain gauge

To save time,
take time to check gauge!

gauge
Flower pot holder: 21 bobbles in pat st = 4 in. (10 cm)

Gold pot holder: 7 repeats of pat st = 4 in. (10 cm)

stitches
Chain (ch), slip st (sl), single crochet (sc), double crochet (dc), bobble

Note: See pages 8–18 for detailed instructions on stitches and shapings.

flower motif
With light green, ch 44 + ch 1 = first st. Row 1: With light green, work 1 sc in the 3rd ch from the hook, 1 sc in each of the foll ch = 44 sts. Row 2: With contrasting color, ch 2 = first st, *in the foll sc, 1 st and 1 bobble (**yo, insert hook and pull up a loop**, work ** to ** twice, yo and draw through 6 loops on hook, yo and draw through 2 loops), skip 1 sc*, rep * to * 20 times, end with 1 dc in the last sc. Row 3: With a 2nd contrasting color, ch 2, 1 sc and 1 bobble between the sc and the bobble of the previous row, work 1 sc and 1 bobble between the foll sc and bobble of the previous row, end with 1 dc in the last st. Row 4: With light green, ch 1, *1 sc in the bobble, 1 sc between the sc and the foll bobble*, rep * to *, end with 1 sc in the last st. Row 5: With light green, ch 1 = first sc, 1 sc in each of the foll sc. Rep rows 2 to 5 until piece measures 7 in. (18 cm), end with the 4th row = 1 row of sc in light green. Do not fasten off, but work 2 sc in the last st, along 1

gold pot holder

Ch 57 + ch 3 = first dc. Row 1: Work 3 dc in the 4th ch from the hook, *skip ch, 3 dc in the foll ch*, rep * to *, end by skipping ch 3, 1 dc in the last ch. Row 2: Ch 3, *3 dc in the underlying ch of the foundation ch between the groups of sc of the previous row*, rep * to *, end with 1 dc in the last st. Row 3: Ch 3, *3 dc in the center dc of the underlying group of dc of the previous row*, rep * to *, end with 1 dc in the last st. The groups of dc are staggered every row. Rep the 3rd row until pot holder measures 7-1/4 in. (18.5 cm). Do not fasten off, but work 1 row of sc around pot holder as foll: Ch 14 for loop, 1 sc in the corner, work in sc around edges, working 3 sc in each corner st. Work 1 sc in each ch of the loop, sl st in the sc after the loop. Fasten off.

side, work 1 row of sc. Fasten off. Join yarn to beg of 2 side edges and work 1 row of sc. Do not fasten off, but work around entire pot holder with 1 row of sc. Ch 14 for loop, work 1 sc in each sc, in the rem 3 corners, work 3 sc in same st. Work 1 sc in each ch of loop, sl 1 in the sc after the loop. Fasten off.

Embroider flowers and leaves by foll sketch. Embroider the flowers and leaves in satin st. Embroider the centers first in satin st with black, then a few large sts in white.

$\mathcal{F}$riendly fish

level
Intermediate

finished measurement
Length: 12 in. (30 cm)

materials
- Mayflower Cotton 8 - Sport weight yarn (approx. 186 yds per 50 g skein) 1 skein each color light blue, blue, dark blue, light pink, pink, and red
- Crochet hook U.S. size C/2 (Metric size 2.5) or size needed to obtain gauge

To save time,
take time to check gauge!

gauge
12 sc and 14 rows = 2 in. (5 cm)

stitches
Chain (ch), slip st (sl), single crochet (sc)

Note: See pages 8–18
for detailed instructions
on stitches and shapings.

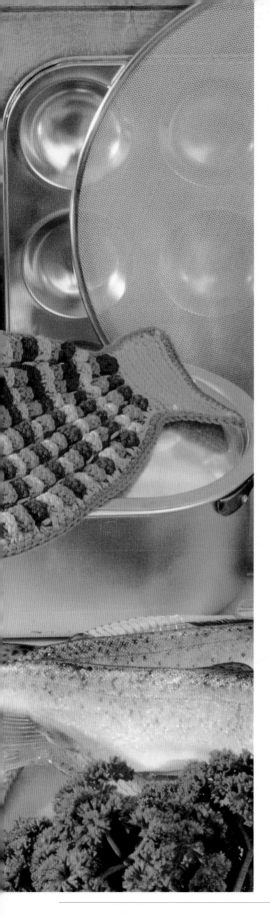

directions

Beg with nose. With crochet hook and light blue, ch 4. Row 1: 1 sc in 3rd ch from hook, 1 sc in the 4th ch from hook. Row 2: Ch 1, 1 sc in first sc, sc in next sc, 2 sc in last sc = 5 sc. Row 3: Ch 1, 1 sc in each of the foll sc, 2 sc in the last st = 7 sc. Inc 1 st at each edge in this manner until you have 25 sts. Work 1 row without incs = 13 rows. Work the small scales as foll: Row 1: Ch 1 = first sc, *ch 2, skip 2 sc, 1 sc*, rep * to * = 8 arcs of ch 2. Row 2: Ch 1, *3 dc in the ch-2 arc, 1 sc*, rep * to *. Row 3: With blue, ch 1, *ch 2, 1 sc*, rep * to *. Row 4: Like row 2. Rows 5 and 6: With dark blue, work like rows 3 and 4. Rows 7 and 8: Like rows 2 and 3 with light blue. Now work larger scales. Row 9: With blue, ch 1 = first sc, ch 3, 1 sc*, rep * to *. Row 10: Ch 1, *4 dc in the ch-3 arc, 1 sc*, rep * to *. Rep the last 2 rows 7 times, then reverse order of colors, working dark blue, light blue, and blue. The last color is dark blue. Work the 3rd and 4th row 3 times for small scales. Row 31: Like row 3. Row 32: Ch 1, *2 dc in the ch-2 arc, 1 sc*, rep * to *. Work the last 2 rows twice. Row 37: Ch 1, *ch 2, skip 2 scales and work 1 sc*, rep * to * = 4 arcs of ch 2. Row 38: Like row 2 of the small scales. Work rows 3 and 4 twice = 4 small scales wide. Row 43: With light blue, ch 1, *ch 1, 1 sc*, rep * to *. Row 44: Ch 1, *2 sc in the ch-2 arc, 1 sc in the sc*, rep * to * = 13 sc. Continue sc in light blue, inc 1 st at each edge of every row. Work 10 rows in sc, inc at each edge = 31 sc. Work 1 round in sc in light blue around the fish, making a loop at point of nose (ch 19). Work 1 round of sc with blue, including sc in loop sts. Fasten off. Embroider eyes and mouth using photo as a guide. Make pink fish in same manner, using shades of pink.

$\mathscr{P}$ink petals

level
Intermediate

finished measurement
Diameter: 8 in. (20 cm)

materials
- Mayflower Cotton 8 - Sport weight yarn (approx. 186 yds per 50 g skein) 1 skein each color green, pink, white, and yellow
- Crochet hook U.S. size C/2 (Metric size 2.5) or size needed to obtain gauge

*To save time,
take time to check gauge!*

gauge
24 sts and 11 rows = 4 in. (10 cm)

stitches
Chain (ch), slip st (sl), single crochet (sc), double crochet (dc)

Jacquard St: Work in rounds, sl st to join at beg of each round. Beg rounds in sc with ch 1 and beg rounds of dc with ch 3. Work with 2 colors by laying the unused color above the previous round and crocheting around it. Work the last loop of the last st of one color with the color of the next st. The pot holder with 11

petals and the pot holder with 8 petals are worked the same through the 6th round. Rounds 7-14 are given for the pot holder with 11 petals with the number of sts between the petals indicated for both the 11 and 8 petal pot holders. Rounds 15-17 are the same for both pot holders.

Note: See pages 8–18 for detailed instructions on stitches and shapings.

directions

With crochet hook and white, ch 6 and sl st to join in a ring. Round 1: With white, 9 sc in ring. Round 2: 2 sc in each sc = 18 sc, sl st to join. Round 3: Sc, working 2 sc in every 2nd sc = 27 sc. Round 4: With yellow and white, work as foll: *2 dc with white, 2 dc with yellow in the foll sc*, rep * to * = 2 yellow and white sts repeated 9 times = 36 dc. Round 5: With white, work in sc, work 2 sc in every 4th dc = 45 sc. Round 6: With pink, work in sc, inc 2 sc around. Round 7: With pink, work in dc, inc 8 (9) dc around = 55 (56) dc. Round 8: With pink and green in dc, work 1 green dc, 6 (8) pink dc, work these 6 (8) dc above a group of 5 (7) dc of the previous round and work green dc between these groups of the previous round = 11 (8) petals = 77 (72) dc. Round 9: Above the green

dc,1 green dc and above each group of 6 (8) pink dc, work 8 (11) dc so that you have increased 2 (3) dc above each petal = 99 (96) dc. Round 10: Work in green above green sts and pink above pink sts, but above the green dc, work 2 (3) dc = 110 (112) dc. Round 11: Above the groups of 2 (3) green dc, work 3 (7) green dc and above the groups of 8 (11) pink dc work 9 pink dc = 132 (128) dc. Round 12: Above the groups of 3 (7) green dc, work 5 (10) green dc and above the 9 pink dc work 7 pink dc = 132 (136) dc. Round 13: In the first and last green dc of each group work 3 dc so that there are 5 (10) dc. Above the 7 pink dc: 5 dc worked tog, by not drawing through the last loop of each st so that after working 5 dc there are 6 loops on the hook. Yo and draw through all loops. Between each group of 11 (16) green dc, work 5 pink dc tog = 132 (136) dc. Round 14: With green, sc, working 2 sc in every 6th dc = 154 (158) sc. Round 15: With green, sc, working 2 sc in every 14th sc = 165 (169) sc. Round 16: With green, sc in back loop only. Round 17: Sc, but work in the back loop of the 15th round. Sl st to join and make a chain 4 in. (10 cm) long and sl st to join in first ch. Work 1 row of sc in chain. Fasten off. Block pot holder.

Light pink motif

level

Intermediate

finished measurement

7 in. (18 cm) square

materials

• Mayflower Cotton 8 - Sport weight yarn (approx. 186 yds per 50 g skein) 1 skein color light pink.

• Crochet hook U.S. size B/1 (Metric size 2.5) or size needed to obtain gauge.

To save time, take time to check gauge!

gauge

33 sts in pat st = 4 in. (10 cm) wide

stitches

Chain (ch), slip st (sl), single crochet (sc)

Note: See pages 8–18 for detailed instructions on stitches and shapings.

directions

Ch 58 + ch 1 to turn. Row 1: 1 sc in the 3rd ch from the hook, *ch 1, skip 1 ch, 1 sc in the foll ch*, rep * to *. Row 2: Ch 1 = first sc, *1 sc around the ch, ch 1, skip 1 sc*, rep * to *, end with 1 sc in the last st. Rep the 2nd row until piece measures 7 in. (18 cm). Do not fasten off, but work 1 row sc around pot holder. Ch 14 in the corner for a loop, 1 sc in the corner and work around edges, working 3 sc in each corner st. Work 1 sc in each ch of the loop, sl 1 in the sc after the loop. Fasten off.

Contrasting colors

level

Intermediate

finished measurement

7-1/2 in. (19 cm) square

materials

• Mayflower Cotton 8 - Sport weight yarn (approx. 186 yds per 50 g skein) 1 skein color each light green and any desired contrasting colors

• Crochet hook U.S. size B/1 (Metric size 2.5) or size needed to obtain gauge

*To save time,
take time to check gauge!*

gauge

1 repeat of pat st = 1-1/4 in. (3 cm) wide

stitches

Chain (ch), slip st (sl), single crochet (sc), double crochet (dc)

Jacquard St: When changing colors, work the last loop of the last st with the color of the next st.

*Note: See pages 8–18
for detailed instructions
on stitches and shapings.*

directions

multicolored motif

With light green, ch 49 + ch 1 to turn. Row 1: With first desired color, work 1 sc in the 2nd ch from the hook, *skip 3 ch sts of the foundation ch, 6 dc in the foll ch = wave, skip 3 ch, 1 sc in the foll ch*, rep * to * 5 times. Row 2: With a 2nd contrasting color, ch 3, work 3 dc tog (1 dc in each of the foll 3 dc of the wave of the previous row, do not complete the 3 dc, yo, draw through the 4 loops on the hook), *ch 3, 1 sc between the 3rd and the 4th dc of the wave, ch 3, 6 dc tog (1 dc in each of the last 3 dc of one wave and 1 dc in each of the first 3 dc of the foll wave, do not complete these 6 dc, yo, draw through 7 loops on the hook),* rep * to *, end last rep with 3 dc tog, 1 dc in the last sc. Row 3: With desired color, ch 3, 3 dc in the 3 dc worked tog, *1 sc in the foll sc, 6 dc in the foll dc worked tog*, rep * to *, end with the last rep with 3 dc in the 3 dc tog, 1 dc in the last st. Row 4: With desired color, ch 1, 1 sc in the last dc of the previous row, *ch 3, 6 dc tog, ch 3, 1 sc between the 3rd and 4th dc of the wave*, rep * to *, end last rep with 1 sc in the last st. Row 5: With desired color, ch 1, 1 sc in the last sc of the previous row, *6 dc in the 6 dc tog, 1 sc in the foll sc*, rep * to *. Row 6: With light green ch 1, 1 sc in each of the foll dc. Row 7: Join desired color at the beg of the 6th row. Ch 3, 3 dc worked tog (1 dc in each of the first 3 sc of the row), ch 3, *1 sc in the foll sc, ch 3, 6 dc worked tog (1 dc in each of the foll 6 sc), ch 3*, rep * to *, end the last rep with 3 dc worked tog, 1 dc in the last sc. Row 8: Work in same color as the 3rd row. Rows 9 and 10: Work in the same color as rows 4 and 5. Row 11: With light green work same as the 6th row. Rows 12 and 13: Work same as rows 7 and 8. Rows 14 and 15: Work same as rows 4 and 5. Rows 16 and 17: Work same as 2nd and 3rd rows. Row 18: With light green, work same as 6th row. Row 19: Join at beg of row 18 with the desired color. 1 sc, *ch 3, 6 dc worked tog (work 1 dc in each of the foll sc), ch 3, 1 sc in the foll sc*, rep * to *. Row 20: Work in the same color as the 5th row. Rows 21 and 22: Work in desired color same as the 2nd and 3rd rows. Row 23: Work in desired color same as on row 4. Fasten off. Join with light green in the first st of the first row. Work along the first side edge, top edge, 2nd side, and lower edge in sc, working 3 sc in each corner st. Work 1 row in sc, ch 14 in the first corner and in the rem corners work 3 sc. Work 1 sc in each ch of the loop, sl st in the sc after the loop. Fasten off.

Red, white & blue

level
Intermediate

finished measurement
7-1/2 in. (19 cm) square

materials
• Mayflower Cotton Helarsgarn - Worsted weight yarn (approx. 86 yds per 50 g skein) 1 skein each color blue or red and white

• Crochet hook U.S. size F/5 (Metric size 4) or size needed to obtain gauge

To save time, take time to check gauge!

gauge
16-1/2 sc and 12-1/2 rows = 4 in. (10 cm)

stitches

Chain (ch), slip st (sl), single crochet (sc), double crochet (dc), front relief dc: work like dc, but work around the front post of the underlying sts.

Jacquard St: Foll chart in hdc. Beg each row with ch 2. When changing colors, work the last loop of the last st with the color of the next st.

Pattern st: multiple of 2 sts + 1.

Row 1: Ch 2 = first sc, 1 sc in the 4th ch from the hook, 1 sc in each of the foll ch.

Row 2: Ch 3 = first dc, 1 dc in each of the foll sc.

Row 3: Ch 1 to turn (doesn't count as first st), 1 sc in the last dc of the previous row, *1 deep front relief dc around the sc of row 1 (2 rows below), skip the dc of the previous row behind that relief dc, 1 sc in the foll dc*, rep * to *. Row 4: Ch 3 = first dc, *1 dc in the foll relief dc, 1 dc in foll sc*, rep * to *. Row 5: Ch 1 to turn, 1 sc in the last dc of the previous row = first st, *1 deep front relief dc around the underlying relief st 2 rows below, skip the dc of the previous row behind the relief dc, 1 sc in the foll dc*, rep * to *. Always rep the 4th and 5th row.

Note: See pages 8–18 for detailed instructions on stitches and shapings.

directions

With red or blue, ch 27 + ch 2 = first st. Row 1: 1 sc in the 4th ch from the hook, 1 sc in each of the foll 25 ch = 27 sc. Work these 27 sts in pat st, beg with the 2nd row. Alternately work 2 rows of red or blue and 2 rows in white. Work 21 rows for back side, end with the 5th row. Work 1 round of sc, working a loop of 12 ch sts in 1 corner and work 3 sc in each of the other 3 corners. Fasten off. With white, work 1 round of sc in red or blue, work 1 sc in each of the 12 ch sts of loop and 3 sc in the 3 corners. Fasten off.

Daisies

The fresh look of a field of daisies lends its magic to this delightful collection of kitchen gifts. There's an oversized daisy pot holder, delicate daisy shelf edging and napkin rings, and crisp yellow and white hand towels. Crochet the entire cheerful set for someone special.

Daisy pot holder

level
Intermediate

finished measurement
Diameter: 7 in. (18 cm)

materials
• Mayflower Cotton Helarsgarn - Worsted weight yarn (approx. 86 yds per 50 g skein) 1 skein each color white and yellow
• Crochet hook U.S. size E/4 (Metric size 3.5) or size needed to obtain gauge

stitches
Chain (ch), slip st (sl), single crochet (sc)

Jacquard St: Foll chart in hdc. Beg each row with ch 2. When changing colors, work the last loop of the last st with the color of the next st. Use small bobbins of yarn for each section of color.

Note: See pages 8–18 for detailed instructions on stitches and shapings.

directions
Worked in rounds, without slip stitching to join unless noted. Mark beg of round. For each pot holder, make 6 circles in main color as foll: ch 4, sl st to join a ring. Round 1: 8 sc in ring. Round 2: 2 sc in each sc = 16 sc. Round 3: 2 sc in every 2nd sc = 24 sc. Round 4: 2 sc in every 3rd sc, evenly spacing incs around. Round 5: 32 sc, end with 1 sl st to join to beg of round. Fasten off. Make 6 circles and lay in a circle and join inner edges tog. Along the outside edges of each circle, leave 18 sts unworked at the top, and 6 sts unworked at the inner edge, and sew 4 sts tog at the juncture. Work the center circle in 2 colors as foll: Rounds 1 to 4: Work same as small circle. Round 5: *3 sc, 2 sc in the foll sc*, rep * to * = 40 sc. Round 6: *1 sc, 2 sc in the foll sc, 3 sc*, rep * to * = 48 sc. End round with 1 sl st in main color. Round 7: Work in back loops of sts: ch 1 = first sc, 47 sc. Work in rounds. Round 8: *1 sc, 1 picot = ch 3, 1 sc in the 3rd ch from the hook, skip 1 sc, 6 sc*, rep * to * = 6 picots. Sl st to join in ring. Fasten off. Place the center circle over the 6 smaller circles with picots placed between them. Sew together using main color. Between 2 smaller circles, with contrasting color, make a 20-chain loop and sew between 2 small circles on wrong side. See photo.

Hand towels

level
Easy

finished measurement
16 x 16 in. (40 x 40 cm)

materials
• Mayflower Cotton 8 - Sport weight yarn (approx. 186 yds per 50 g skein) 1 skein each color white and yellow

• Crochet hook U.S. size B/1 (Metric size 2.5) or size needed to obtain gauge

To save time, take time to check gauge!

gauge
21 sc and 26 rows = 4 in. (10 cm)

stitches
Chain (ch), slip st (sl), single crochet (sc)

Note: See pages 8–18 for detailed instructions on stitches and shapings.

directions
Ch 84 + ch 1 to turn = first sc. Row 1: Work in sc, beg first sc in the 3rd ch from the hook and work 1 sc in foll 82 ch sts. Continue in sc. Ch 1 to turn = 1 sc. Work until piece measures 16 in. (40 cm). Ch 16 at end of last row for loop. Sl st to join. Fasten off. With contrasting color, work 1 row of sc around edges and loop, working 3 sc in each corner st. Fasten off.

Daisy shelf edging & napkin rings

level
Intermediate

finished measurement
Length: 39 in. (100 cm)

materials
- Mayflower Cotton 8 - Sport weight yarn (approx. 180 yds per 50 g skein) 1 skein each color white and yellow
- Steel crochet hook U.S. size 4 (Metric size 2) or size needed to obtain gauge

stitches
Chain (ch), slip st (sl), single crochet (sc), double crochet (dc)

2 dc worked tog: Work the first dc until 2 loops on hook, work the 2nd dc until 3 loops are on hook, draw through loops on hook.

3 dc worked tog: Work the first dc until 2 loops rem on hook, work the 2nd dc until 3 loops are on hook, work the 3rd dc until 4 loops are on hook, draw through loops on hook.

Flower motif: With yellow (white), ch 4 and sl st to join in a ring. Round 1: Ch 8 sc in a ring, ch 1 = first sc. Sl st in a ring with the foll color (for the flower petals). Round 2: With white(yellow), ch 1 = 1 sc, *2 sc in the foll sc, 1 sc in the foll sc*, rep * to *, end with 2 sc in the last sc. Sl st to join in a ring = 12 sc. Round 3: Ch 2, 2 dc worked tog in the sl st, ch 3, 1 sl st in the foll sc, *ch 3, 3 dc worked tog in the foll sc, ch 3, sl st in the foll sc*, rep * to * 4 times, end round with ch 3, 1 sl st in the 2nd ch from the beg. Fasten off = 6 flower petals.

Note: See pages 8–18 for detailed instructions on stitches and shapings.

directions

edging
Make 24 flowers with yellow centers and white petals or white centers and yellow petals. Leave a strand hanging from each flower. Sew the flowers together, petal to petal, so that 2 petals are unsewn at top and bottom. Along the upper edge of petals in contrasting color of petals, work as foll: join yarn at outside petal of top edge at right side. Row 1: *1 sc in the dc worked tog, ch 6, 1 sc of the dc worked tog, ch 6*, rep * to *, end with ch 6, 1 sc in the last petal at the left edge. Row 2: Ch 4 to turn, *1 sc in the center of the ch-6 arc, ch 5*, rep * to * around each of the foll ch-6 arcs and end with sl st in the sc at the beg of row 1. Fasten off. Block piece to indicated measurement.

napkin rings
Make 1 flower with a yellow center and white petals. After the last petal, ch 15 and sl st to opposite petal to join in ring.

Cover-ups

Cotton afghan

This lovely cotton afghan, with its graceful pattern and natural color, would complement any room decor.

level
Intermediate

finished measurement
45 x 60 in. (112 x 150 cm)

materials
- Ruby Mills' Create-It (approx. 89 yds per 50 g skein) 32 skeins undyed - color ecru
- Crochet hook U.S. size F/5 (Metric size 4) or size needed to obtain gauge

To save time, take time to check gauge!

gauge
12 dc and 10 rows = 4 in. (10 cm)

stitches
Chain (ch), slip st (sl), single crochet (sc), double crochet (dc)

Note: See pages 8–18 for detailed instructions on stitches and shapings.

panel 1
Ch 182. Row 1: 1 dc in the 4th ch from hook, 1 dc in each ch = 180 dc. Ch 1 to turn. Row 2: Sc in first st, *skip 1 st, 1 sc in next st, 1 bobble worked in sc just worked as foll: **yo, insert hook in st, yo, draw up loop**, rep ** to ** 3 times in same st = 7 loops on hook, yo and draw through 6 loops = 2 loops on hook, yo and draw through 2 loops*, rep * to *, end with 1 dc in last st. Ch 1 to turn. Row 3: Sc in first dc, *skip bobble and work 1 sc and bobble in next sc*, rep * to * across, end with 1 dc in last st. Ch 3 to turn. Row 4: Dc in each st across = 180 dc. Ch 3 to turn. Repeat row 4, 4 times. Work rows 2 and 3 once. Repeat row 4, 5 times. Work rows 2 and 3 once. Repeat row 4, 5 times. Work rows 2 and 3 once. Rep row 4, 3 times. Ch 3 to turn.

panel 2
Work in last row of panel 1. Row 1: 1 dc in first 12 dc, ch 1, skip 1 dc, *1 dc in next 12 dc, ch 1, skip 1 dc, 1 dc in next st*, rep * to * to end. Ch 3 to turn. Row 2: *1 dc in 11 dc, ch 1, skip 1 dc, 1 dc in next st, ch 1, skip 1 dc, 1 dc in next ch, skip 1 dc, 1 dc,* rep * to *. Work next row the same way, adding 1 open square at each edge of each open motif until there are 5 open squares, then work 2nd half to correspond by eliminating 1 open square at each edge of each motif. Work 2 rows of dc.

panel 3
Ch 3 to turn. Work in last row of panel 2. Row 1: 1 dc in 3rd ch from hook, ch 1, *skip 1 dc, 1 dc in next dc, ch 1*, rep * to *. Ch 3 to turn. Row 2: Work puff st in 1 ch-1 space: yo, draw up loop 4 times, yo, draw through 9 loops on hook, ch 1 to close. Work puff st in next ch-1 space. Repeat rows 1 and 2, 9 times. Work 1 row as foll: *Ch 4, 1 dc, skip 1 dc, 1 dc in next dc,* rep * to * to end of row. Work 2 rows of dc.

Work 2nd half of afghan by working panel 2, then panel 1, working from last row to first row to rev design. Fasten off.

finishing
Cut 182 strands 1-yard (1 m) long. Fold in half twice. Pull folded strand through sts at end of each row. Pass strands through loop and knot. Trim straight across.

Block afghan

Easy to make and easy to love describe this colorful afghan crocheted with blocks of soft mohair. Colors can be easily adapted to match particular rooms.

level

Easy

finished measurement

Width: 56 in. (140 cm)

Length: 72 in. (180 cm)

Each block is 8 x 8 in. (20 x 20 cm)

materials

- Mohair yarn (50 g skein) 4 skeins each color dark gray, light gray, blue, and yellow, 6 skeins color pink, and 7 skeins color green
- Crochet hook U.S. size J/10 (Metric size 6) or size needed to obtain gauge
- Yarn needle
- Nylon brush

To save time, take time to check gauge!

gauge

14 sc and 17 rows = 4 in. (10 cm)

stitches

Chain (ch), single crochet (sc)

Note: See pages 8–18 for detailed instructions on stitches and shapings.

directions

Make 63 blocks and join with hem stitch. Block: Ch 28 + ch 1 = first sc. Row 1: 1 sc in the 3rd ch from the hook, 1 sc in each of the foll ch = 28 sc. Row 2: Ch 1 = first sc, 1 sc in each of the foll sc, 1 sc in ch at the corner. Rep the 2nd row to a height of 8 in. (20 cm). Fasten off. Make 9 light gray, dark gray, blue, and yellow blocks, 13 pink and 14 green blocks = 63 blocks.

finishing

Block pieces to indicated measurements. Lay the blocks foll the chart: 7 blocks wide and 9 blocks long. Sew tog with green yarn in hem stitch. Brush the mohair with a nylon brush.

hem stitch

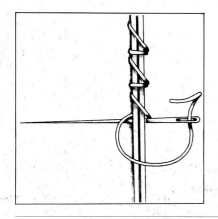

block chart

1	2	5	1	2	1	6
5	6	2	5	6	5	3
1	3	4	1	2	1	4
3	5	1	5	4	6	5
5	1	4	6	1	4	3
1	2	5	3	5	1	2
2	5	6	4	6	4	6
3	4	2	3	1	5	3
1	6	5	4	3	2	1

KEY TO CHART

1 = green

2 = dark gray

3 = light gray

4 = blue

5 = pink

6 = yellow

Yellow bedspread

Intricate openwork, time-less design, and subdued color give this bedspread the look of an heirloom.

level

Experienced

finished measurement

50 x 80 in. (125 x 200 cm), 60 x 80 in. (150 x 200 cm), 70 x 80 in. (175 x 200 cm)

Each block: 10 x 10 in. (25 x 25 cm)

materials

- Mayflower Cotton 8 - Sport weight yarn (approx. 186 yds per 50 g skein) 29 (34, 40) skeins color yellow

- Crochet hook U.S. size C/2 (Metric size 2.5) or size needed to obtain gauge

To save time, take time to check gauge!

gauge

13 squares and 10-1/2 rows = 4 in. (10 cm)

stitches

Chain (ch), slip st (sl), single crochet (sc), double crochet (dc)

Picot: Ch 3, 1 sc in 3rd ch from hook

2 dc worked tog: Work the first dc until 2 loops rem on hook, then work the 2nd dc until 3 loops rem on hook, yo and draw through all loops.

Note: See pages 8–18 for detailed instructions on stitches and shapings.

directions

Each block is 32 squares and 26 rows high and worked by foll chart. The first row of each block is open squares. Work as foll: Ch 73 + ch 4 = first open square. Row 1: 1 dc in 7th ch from hook, *ch 1, skip 1, 1 dc in next st*, rep * to *. Work by foll each chart 5 (6, 7) times = 40 (48, 56) blocks total. Fasten off.

finishing

Block pieces to indicated measurements. Place blocks as shown on chart. Make 5 (6, 7) panels of 8 blocks as foll: make a chain 14 in. (35 cm) long and sew with over-hand st the last row of open squares of one block to the first row of open squares of the foll block. Fasten off. Continue in this way until 8 squares are joined tog. Make a chain about 92 in. (2.3 m) long and sew left side edge of panel to right edge of 2nd panel. When all panels are sewn tog, work 1 round of sc around outside edge. Work 2 sc in each square. In each square at top and lower edge, work 1 sc in each square and 3 sc in each corner. Sl st to join. Fasten off.

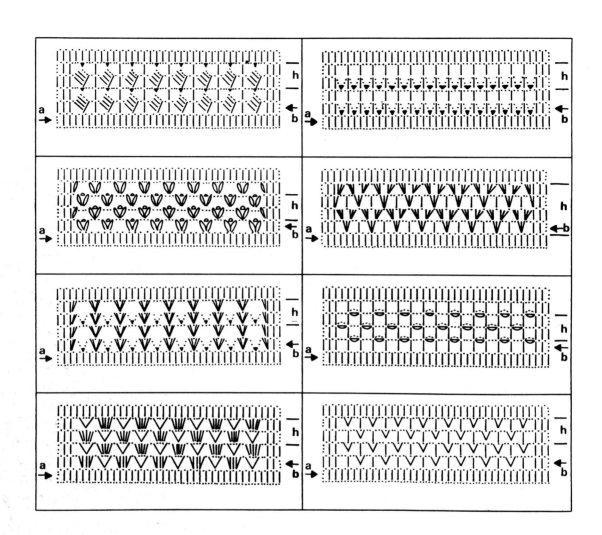

KEY TO CHART

⬝	=	ch
▼	=	sc
‖	=	dc
⬭	=	work as foll: work 2 dc tog: in the ch and the foll dc, 1 picot, 2 dc worked tog: in the same dc and the foll ch.
⬭	=	2 dc worked tog in the underlying ch arc.
⌒	=	picot
☺	=	ch 3, 2 dc worked tog in the 3rd ch from the hook.
a	=	beg first row
b	=	beg 2nd row
h	=	repeat

block chart

1	6	3	8	5	2	7
2	7	4	1	6	3	8
3	8	5	2	7	4	1
4	1	6	3	8	5	2
5	2	7	4	1	6	3
6	3	8	5	2	7	4
7	4	1	6	3	8	5
8	5	2	7	4	1	6

10

80

70

60

50

and-dyed scarf

The secret to this stunning scarf is the bulky, hand-dyed yarn in variegated colors that crochets quickly into naturally nubby stripes. It looks great on a man or woman.

level
Easy

finished measurement
9 x 56 in. (22 x 140 cm)

materials
- Bulky weight hand-dyed varie-gated yarn 16 oz color turquoise and violet
- Crochet hook U.S. size K/10.25 (Metric size 7) or size needed to obtain gauge

To save time, take time to check gauge!

gauge
9 sc and 5-1/2 rows = 4 in. (10 cm)

stitches
Chain (ch), single crochet (sc)

Note: See pages 8–18 for detailed instructions on stitches and shapings.

directions
Cut 42 strands 20 in. (50 cm) long for fringe and put aside. Ch 22, sc in 2nd ch from hook, sc across = 21 sc. Ch 1, turn, 21 sc. Continue until all yarn is used. Attach fringe to ends by folding in half and knotting.

Scarf & beret

Dappled autumn hues contrast handsomely with heathery teal in this wool scarf and beret set. It will make a welcome present when the leaves turn gold and red.

level
Intermediate

finished measurement
Hat: average head size

Scarf: 8 x 52 in. (20 x 132 cm)

materials
• Alice Starmore - Worsted weight yarn (approx. 120 yds per 2 oz skein) 3 skeins color night hawk, MC, 2 skeins color autumn, CC

• Crochet hook U.S. size H/8 (Metric size 5) or size needed to obtain gauge

To save time, take time to check gauge!

gauge
12 hdc and 12 rows = 4 in. (10 cm)

stitches
Chain (ch), slip st (sl), single crochet (sc), half double crochet (hdc)

Jacquard St: Foll chart in hdc. Beg each row with ch 2. When changing colors, work the last loop of the last st with the color of the next st.

Note: See pages 8–18 for detailed instructions on stitches and shapings.

Beret

With MC, ch 4 and sl st to join in a ring. Do not sl st to join unless otherwise indicated. Round 1: 8 hdc in ring. Round 2: Work 2 hdc in each st. Round 3: Hdc, working 2 hdc in every 2nd st. Round 4: Hdc, working 2 hdc in every 3rd st. Round 5: Hdc, working 2 hdc in every 4th st. Continue in this way working 1 more hdc between incs on each round. Keep inc above ones on previous rounds. After the 12th round you should have 96 hdc. Work 12 rounds even. Dec as foll: *dec 1 (draw thru a loop in one st, draw thru a loop in next st, draw thru 3 loops on hook), 3 hdc*, rep * to * 7 times, **dec 1, 2hdc, dec 1, 3 hdc**, rep ** to ** 6 times, ***dec 1, 2 hdc, dec 1, 1 hdc***, rep *** to ***11 times. Work 10 rows even as foll: 1 row in CC, 1 row in MC. Fasten off.

finishing
Fold these 10 rows in half to outside and sl st in place. The wrong side of work forms the right side of beret.

Scarf

With MC, ch 160. Row 1: Hdc in 3rd ch from hook and in each ch across = 158 hdc. Turn. Continue in hdc as foll: 2 more rows in MC, 2 rows in CC, 2 rows in MC, 9 rows in CC, 2 rows in MC, 2 rows in CC, 3 rows in MC. Fasten off.

finishing
Make fringe in corresponding colors and attach to each end.

Child's hat & scarf

The deep ribbing in this hat and scarf set gives it a thick and plush feel, perfect for keeping kids warm and dry. (High-quality acrylic yarn makes for easy care for moms and dads.)

level

Intermediate

finished measurement

Hat: 15 (18) in.—38 (46) cm

Scarf: 6 x 43 in. (15 x 109 cm) not including fringe

materials

- Chunky weight acrylic yarn (approx. 165 yds per 100 g skein) 2 skeins each color solid turquoise, MC and tweedy turquoise, CC
- Crochet hook U.S. size I/8 (Metric size 5.5) or size needed to obtain gauge

To save time, take time to check gauge!

gauge

17 relief dc and 9 rows = 4 in. (10 cm)

stitches

Chain (ch), slip st (sl), single crochet (sc), double crochet (dc)

Front Relief dc: Dc working around front of vertical post of st in previous row

Back Relief dc: Dc working around back of verical post of st in previous row. Beg each row with ch 2. When changing colors, work the last loop of the last st with the color of the next st.

Note: See pages 8–18 for detailed instructions on stitches and shapings.

Hat

With MC, ch 4, sl st to join in ring. Round 1: Right side: Ch 3 = first dc, 15 (18) dc in ring. Round 2: Inc round: Ch 3, front relief dc around vertical post of same st, *dc in next st, front relief dc around vertical post of same st*, rep * to *, sl st to join = 30 (36) sts. Round 3: Same as round 2 = 60 (72) sts. Round 4: Ch 3, 2 front relief dc, *1 back relief dc, 2 front relief dc*, rep * to *, sl st to join. Rounds 5 and 6: Same as round 4. Rounds 7 - 9: With CC, same as round 4. Rounds 10 - 18 (20): With MC, same as round 4.

Band: Round 1: Ch 3, turn, back relief dc in each st around. Sl st to join. Round 2: Ch 3, 2 front relief dc, *back relief dc, 2 front relief dc*, rep * to *, sl st to join.

Rounds 3 and 4: With CC, same as round 2. Rounds 5 and 6: With MC, same as round 2. Round 7: With CC, ch 1, sc in same st and in each st around. Round 8: With MC, same as round 7. Fasten off.

finishing

Make a pompom in CC and attach to top of hat.

Scarf

With CC, ch 23. Row 1: Dc in 3rd ch from hook and in each ch across = 22 dc. Turn. Row 2: Ch 2 = first dc, *2 front relief dc, 1 back relief dc*, work * to * 6 times, end with 2 front relief dc, 1 dc. Turn. Row 3: Ch 2 = first dc, *2 back relief dc, 1 front relief dc*, work * to * 6 times, end with 2 back relief dc, 1 dc. Rep rows 2 and 3 as foll: 4 rows in CC, *2 rows in MC, 2 rows in CC* rep * to * 21 times, end with 2 rows in MC, 4 rows in CC. Work 1 row of sc in CC around entire scarf, sl st to join. Fasten off.

finishing

Make fringe along each end, cutting strands 10 in. (25.5 cm) long.

Striped relief-stitch scarf

Who wouldn't want to bundle up in this soft cotton chenille scarf (feels like velvet!), with vibrant colors and pleasing stripes?

level
Intermediate

finished measurement
8 x 46 in. (20 x 115 cm)

materials
- Worsted weight chenille yarn 2 skeins each blue, ocher, navy, slate, fuchsia, and purple
- Crochet hook U.S. size I/9 (Metric size 5.5) or size needed to obtain gauge

To save time, take time to check gauge!

gauge
11 dc and 10 rows = 4 in. (10 cm)

stitches
Chain (ch), double crochet (sc)

Front relief dec: Work same as dc, but insert hook in front post of st in underlying st.

Note: See pages 8–18 for detailed instructions on stitches and shapings.

directions

With blue, ch 22 + ch 3 = first dc. Work 1 dc in 4th ch from hook, dc across = 23 dc. Work in relief pat as foll: Ch 3, *1 front relief dc, 3 dc*, rep * to * 5 times, end with 1 dc. row 2: Ch 1 to turn, 1 sc in each st across = 23 sc. Rep these 2 rows, alternating 2 rows in the foll colors: blue, purple, fuchsia, slate, navy, ocher. Work 9 repeats of color sequence, end in blue. Fasten off. Attach fringe to ends by folding in half and knotting.

In the bag

Cotton satchels

Bold colors, jazzy patterns, and sport-weight yarn make these bags both pretty and practical.

level
Intermediate

finished measurement
Height: 8 in. (20 cm)

materials
- Mayflower Cotton 8 - Sport weight cotton yarn (approx. 186 yds per 50 g skein) 1 skein each color pink, green, orange, and purple
- Crochet hook U.S. size C/2 (Metric size 2.5) or size needed to obtain gauge

To save time, take time to check gauge!

gauge
32 sc and 26 rows = 4 in. (10 cm)

stitches
Chain (ch), slip st (sl), single crochet (sc), double crochet (dc)

Jacquard St: When changing colors, work the last loop of the last st with the color of the next st. Use small bobbins of yarn for each section of color.

Note: See pages 8–18 for detailed instructions on stitches and shapings.

directions

Beg with green (pink), ch 3 and sl st to join in ring. Beg each round with ch 2 instead of 1 sc and end each row with sl st in the 2nd ch from the beg. Round 1: 6 sc in ring. Round 2: Work 2 sc in each sc = 12 sc. Round 3: *1 sc, 2 sc in the foll sc*, rep * to * = 18 sc. Round 4: *2 sc, 2 sc in the foll sc*, rep * to * = 24 sc. Round 5: *3 sc, 2 sc in the foll sc*, rep * to * = 30 sc. Round 6: *4 sc, 2 sc in the foll sc*, rep * to * = 36 sc. Round 7: *5 sc, 2 sc in the foll sc*, rep * to * = 42 sc. Round 8: *6 sc, 2 sc in the foll sc*, rep * to * = 48 sc At the same time, for the pink bag, alternately work 2 sc in pink and 2 sc in green. Round 9: Sc without inc. Round 10: With pink (3 sc in pink, 2 sc in green, inc sts on the pink sts), *1 sc, 2 sc in the foll sc, 1 sc in each of the foll 2 sc*, rep * to * = 60 sc. Round 11: Work in sc, without incs, in corresponding colors. Round 12: In green (3 sc in pink, 3 sc in green, inc sc in the green sts), *4 sc, 2 sc in the foll sc*, rep * to * = 72 sc. Round 13: 4 sc in purple and 4 sc in green(3 sc in pink, 3 sc in green), work in sc without incs. Round 14: 5 sc in purple, 4 sc in green, that is, work 4 sc in purple and work 1 inc in purple = 81 sc (4 sc in pink, 3 sc in green, that is work 1 inc in the 3rd pink st = 84 sc). Round 15: Work without incs in corresponding colors. Round 16: 5 sc in purple, 5 sc in green, that is in every 4th green sc, inc 1 = 90 sc (5 pink sc and 3 green sc, that is inc 1 in every 4th pink sc = 96 sc.) Round 17: Work in sc, without incs, in corresponding colors. Round 18: 6 sc in purple and 5 sc in green, that is , make 1 inc in the last purple st = 99 sc (6 sc in pink, 5 sc in green, that is, inc 1 st in the last pink sc = 108 sc). For the striped bag, work without incs in corresponding colors to the 39th round. Round 19: For the jacquard bag, work without increases in corresponding colors. Round 20: Work in green, evenly spacing 9 sc = 108 sc. Now continue without incs. Rounds 21 and 22: Pink. Rounds 23 and 24: Purple. Round 25: Green. Round 26: 6 sc in pink and 6 sc in green. Rounds 27 to 31: Sc in corresponding colors. Round 32: Green. Rounds 33 and 34: Orange. Rounds 35 and 36: Purple. Round 37: Green. Round 38: For jacquard bag: 6 sc in orange and 6 sc in green around. Rounds 39 to 44: For jacquard bag: Work in corresponding colors. Round 40: For striped bag: 6 sc in pink, 3 sc in green, working every 2nd and 3rd green sc tog = 12 dec = 96 sc. Round 41: For striped bag: 6 sc in pink and 2 sc in green. Round 42: 6 sc in pink and 1 sc in green = 84 sc. Rounds 43 to 47: For striped bag: Green in sc. Round 45: For the jacquard bag: Work in sc in green. Rounds 46 and 47: For the jacquard bag, sc in purple. Round 48: In orange (green), *1 dc in each of the foll 2 sc, ch 1, skip 1*, rep * to *. For the jacquard bag, end with 1 round in orange, 2 rounds in green and 2 rounds in pink in sc. For the striped bag, end with 2 rounds in green, 2 rounds in pink, 2 rounds in green in sc. Fasten off. Make a green chain cord 24 in. (60 cm) long and thread through dc round and tie ends tog.

Cotton hammock & bag

level

Intermediate

finished measurement

Hammock: 36 x 60 in. (90 x 150 cm)

Bag length: 24 in. (60 cm); diameter of bottom: 9-1/2 in. (24 cm)

materials

- Mayflower Cotton Helarsgarn - Worsted weight cotton yarn (approx. 86 yds per 50 g skein) 2 skeins each color khaki, light yellow, yellow, orange, red, bright pink, purple, light blue, blue, and green
- 2 metal rings and a hook
- A metal ring with a diameter of 9-1/2 in. (24 cm)
- Crochet hook U.S. size E/4 (Metric size 3.5) or size needed to obtain gauge

*To save time,
take time to check gauge!*

gauge

4 arcs of 6 chains and 1 sc = 4 in. (10 cm)

stitches

Chain (ch), slip st (sl), single crochet (sc), double crochet (dc)

Note: See pages 8–18 for detailed instructions on stitches and shapings.

Hammock

Worked in 9 bands. With crochet hook and khaki, ch 18. Row 1: 1 sc in the 9th ch from the hook, *ch 6, skip 2 ch, 1 sc in the foll ch*, rep * to * 3 times. Turn. Row 2: *Ch 6, 1 sc in the foll ch-6 arc*, rep * to * 4 times, turn. Repeat the 2nd row until piece measures 60 in. (150 cm) = 100 rows. End with ch 6, 1 sc in the foll arc, ch 2, 1 sc in the foll arc, ch 2, 1 sc in the foll arc, ch 6, 1 sc in the last arc. Fasten off.

second band

With light yellow, join to the 13th ch of the foundation ch of the first band and ch 18. Row 1: 1 sc in the 9th ch from the hook, *ch 6, skip 2 ch, 1 sc*, work * to * 3 times, ch 3 and 1 sc in the first side arc of the first band. Turn. Row 2: *Ch 6, 1 sc in the foll ch-6 arc*, rep * to * 3 times. Turn. Row 3: *Ch 6, 1 sc in the foll ch-6 arc*, rep * to * 3 times, ch 3, 1 sc in the foll side arc of the first band. Turn. Rep the last 2 rows of this band, joining to the first band as on the first row. Fasten off. Make bands in the same way in the foll colors: 3rd band in yellow, 4th band in orange, 5th band in red, 6th band in bright pink, 7th band in purple, 8th band in light blue, 9th band in blue. Fasten off.

border

Along the first band, work in green. Join yarn in the corner. Row 1: Work 1 sc in the first side of arc, *ch 8, 1 sc in the foll side of arc*, rep * to *. Row 2: *Ch 8, 1 sc in the foll arc*, rep * to *. Row 3: Like row 2. Row 4: Ch 4 with green, continue in blue, ch 4, 1 sc in the foll arc, *ch 8, 1 sc in the foll arc*, rep * to *. Row 5: Ch 4 with blue, continue in light blue, ch 4, 1 sc in the foll arc, *ch 8, 1 sc in the foll arc*, rep * to *. Work in the same way in the foll colors: 6th row in purple, 7th row in bright pink, 8th row in red, 9th row in orange, 10th row in yellow, 11th row in light yellow, 12th row in khaki. Fasten off. Work along the other side. Along the blue band work in the same way, but work as foll: 3 rows in green, 1 row in khaki, 1 row in light yellow, 1 row in yellow, 1 row in orange, 1 row in red, 1 row in bright pink, 1 row in purple,

Bright bands of color crocheted in matching stitches create a pleasing gift duo: one's great for resting and the other for carrying.

1 row in light blue, 1 row in blue. Work 1 row along the short side of the 9th band, working 3 sc in each arc and work 1 row of sc in these sts. Work along one side with blue and along the other side in red. See photo.

finishing

Loosely braid 2 green cords with 4 strands 240 in. (6 m) long so that you have 2 cords about 120 in. (3 m) long. Thread these cords through the bands, beg at the center of one narrow side to the center of a long side. Thread the 2nd cord from the center of one long side to the center of the 2nd narrow side. Thread the cords through the outside arcs along the edges. Knot the ends of the cord at center of both short sides. With 10 strands, 1 strand of each color, make 2 chains (using a large hook or your fingers) about 60 in. (1.5 m) long for hanging ties. Thread the ties through each narrow side.

ag

Beg with the bottom. With khaki, ch 6 and sl st to join in ring. Work in dc, beg each round with ch 3 = first dc and end with sl st to join in the 3rd ch from hook. Round 1: Work 16 dc in ring. Round 2: Dc, with 2 dc in every 2nd st = 24 dc. Round 3: Dc, with 2 dc in every 2nd dc = 36 dc. Round 4: Dc with 2 dc in every 2nd dc = 54 dc. Round 5: Dc with 2 dc in every 3rd dc = 72 dc. Round 6: Dc without incs. Round 7: Dc with 2 dc in every 4th dc = 90 dc. Round 8: Dc without incs. Round 9: Dc with 2 dc in every 5th dc = 108 dc. The circle is now the same size as the ring. Lay the ring over the 8th round to measure. Fasten off. Join green in the first dc, *ch 6, skip 2*, rep * to * 36 times. End row with 1 sl st in the sl st near the center of the foll arc. Work 3 rows of arcs with ch 6 and 1 sc in the underlying ch-6 arc. Sl st the last row to the center of the foll arc, but make the last loop with blue. Work 4 rows of arcs with blue, then 4 rows of arcs with light blue, purple, bright pink, red, orange, yellow, and light yellow. Fasten off.

finishing

Make a cord 120 in. (3 m) long with 3 strands of khaki. Fold the cord in half and thread the cord through a round of arcs at top of bag. Sew a small ring and hook to the ends of the cord. Sew the big ring to the edge of the bottom. See photo.

Backpack

This lovely backpack has three features that make it a big hit with shoppers and travelers: capacity, comfort, and convenience.

level

Intermediate

finished measurement

Circumference: 36 in. (90 cm)
Length: 15 in. (38 cm)

materials

• Mayflower Cotton 8 - Sport weight yarn (approx. 186 yds per 50 g skein) 3 skeins color of your choice
• 2 silver rings with 1 straight edge
• 1 silver clasp
• A piece of white leather 3/4 x 3-1/2 in. (2 x 9 cm)
• White cotton fabric 4 x 2-1/2 in. (10 x 6 cm)
• Two cords 2 yds (1.70 m) long
• Crochet hook U.S. size C/2 (Metric size 2.5) or size needed to obtain gauge

*To save time,
take time to check gauge!*

gauge

12 squares = 4 in. (10 cm)

stitches

Chain (ch), slip st (sl), single crochet (sc), double crochet (dc)

Note: See pages 8–18 for detailed instructions on stitches and shapings.

directions

Ch 216 and sl st to join in ring. Work in rounds. Round 1: Ch 4 = first open square, skip 1 ch, 1 dc in the foll ch, *ch 1, skip 1 ch, 1 dc in the foll ch*, rep * to *, end round with sl st in the 3rd ch from the beg = 108 open squares. Round 2: Like round 1, but work dc in the dc. Round 3: 1 sc in the first open square, *ch 6, skip 1 open square, sc*, rep * to *, sl st in the first sc = 54 squares with ch 6 between them. Round 4: Sl st to center of arc, 1 sc in arc, ch 6, *1 sc in foll arc, ch 6*, rep * to *, sl st to join in the first sc. Rep the 4th round until piece measures 14-1/4 in. (36 cm). Foll round: Sl st to center of foll arc, 1 sc in arc, ch 3, *1 sc in the foll arc, ch 3*, rep * to *, sl st in the first sc = 54 arcs with ch 3 between them. Work 2 rounds of open squares as

foll: Round 1: Sl st in the first ch, ch 4, skip 1 ch, 1 dc in the foll ch, *ch 1, skip 1 sc, 1 dc in the foll ch, ch 1, skip 1 ch, 1 dc in the foll ch*, rep * to *, sl st in the 3rd ch of the ch-4 arc = 54 open squares. Round 2: Ch 4, 1 dc in the foll dc, *ch 1, 1 dc in the foll dc*, rep * to *, sl st in the 3rd ch from the beg. Fasten off.

finishing

Sew lower edges tog, leaving 3/4 in. (2 cm) open. Cut 2 rectangles of cotton fabric 2 x 2-1/2 in (5 x 6 cm). Fold each rectangle in half so each rectangle is 1 x 2-1/2 in. (2.5 x 6 cm). Sew along long edge with 1/4 in. (.5 cm) hem. Iron the seam flat and turn right sides tog. Thread the fabric through 1 ring, leaving 1/4 in. (1 cm) flap and sew in place. Make a 2nd piece. Fold 2 cords in half. Knot through ring (see photo). Thread through the 2 rows of open squares at upper edge, beg at center back and end at center front on both sides. Fold the leather around the ends of the cord. Slip through holes of metal buckle and crimp around cords. See photo.

Two-handled bag

Here's a perfect gift for that special someone who wants to save a tree: she can carry home groceries in an attractive and sturdy cotton bag.

level
Intermediate

finished measurement
Height 7 in. (18 cm)

materials
- Worsted weight yarn (approx. 99 yds per 50 g skein) 5 skeins in desired color
- Crochet hook U.S. size E/4 (Metric size 3.5)

stitches
Chain (ch), slip st (sl), single crochet (sc), half double crochet (hdc)

Note: See pages 8–18 for detailed instructions on stitches and shapings.

directions
Ch 6. Sl st to join rounds 1-6. Round 1: 15 dc in ring, sl st to join. Round 2: 2 dc in each dc = 30 dc, sl st to join. Round 3: *1 dc, 2 dc in next dc*, rep * to * = 45 dc. Round 4: *2 dc, 2 dc in next dc*, rep * to * = 60 dc. Round 5: 1 dc, *2 dc in next dc, 3 dc*, rep * to *, end with 2 dc in next dc, 2 dc = 75 dc. Round 6: Work in sc, inc 9 sc around = 84 sc. Now work in rounds for the mesh, but do not sl st to join at end of round: Round 1: *Draw a loop over hook about 1/3 in. (1.5 cm) long, yo and draw through a loop, 1 sc around the back strand of the loop, ch 1*, rep * to * once, then 2 sc above the skipped st, 1 sc, rep from first * = 28 arcs. Rounds 2 to 17: *Draw a loop over hook about 1/3 in. (1.5 cm) long, yo and draw through a loop, 1 sc around the back strand of the loop, ch 1*, rep * to * once, 1 sc in the top sc of the previous arc, insert hook in the underlying horizontal loop of the group, rep from first *. Above the 17th round, work as foll: ch 4, 1 sc in the top sc of the foll arc, rep from first *. Sl st to join. Work 3 rounds of sc and fasten off. Handles: Make 2 chains about 11-1/2 in. (29 cm) long, work 3 rows sc, beg each row with ch 2 for the first sc. Sew handles spaced 4 loops apart at each side of the bag.

Kids' stuff

Rabbit pullover

Delight a special friend with this adorable rabbit pullover. The design, with its trio of overall-clad rabbits (complete with embroidered whiskers!) and crop of carrots, is sure to make a welcome gift.

level

Intermediate

size

Child's size 2-3 years, chest 21, 23 in. (52.5, 57.5 cm)

finished measurement

Chest: 25-1/2 in. (64 cm)

Length: 13-1/4 in. (33 cm)

Sleeve seam: 9-1/2 in. (24 cm)

materials

- Sport weight yarn (approx. 150 yds per 50 g skein) 3 skeins color blue, 1 skein each color green, orange, red, gray, and white
- 4 orange buttons
- Crochet hook U.S. size E/4 (Metric size 3.5) or size needed to obtain gauge
- Knitting needles U.S. size 4 (Metric size 3.5)

To save time,
take time to check gauge!

gauge

18 hdc and 13 rows = 4 in. (10 cm)

stitches

Chain (ch), slip st (sl), single crochet (sc), half double crochet (hdc)

Jacquard St: Foll chart in hdc. Beg each row with ch 2. When

changing colors, work the last loop of the last st with the color of the next st. Use small bobbins of yarn for each section of color.

1/1 ribbing: Row 1: *K1, p1*. Rep * to * across. Row 2 and all foll rows: Work sts as established in previous row.

Note: See pages 8–18 for detailed instructions on stitches and shapings.

back

With crochet hook and green, ch 59 + ch 2 = first hdc. Work the first hdc in the 4th ch from the hook. Rows 1 and 2: Hdc in green = 59 hdc. Row 3: Right side facing, first row of chart: ch 2 in blue, *3 hdc in orange, 3 hdc in blue*, rep * to * 9 times, end after the last rep with 3 hdc in orange, 1 hdc in blue = 10 zig-zags. Continue by foll chart. When piece measures 6 in. (15 cm) from beg = 19 rows, leave 6 sts unworked at each edge for armholes. Work center 47 sts until armhole measures 5 in. (12.5 cm) = 16 rows. Leave the center 15 sts unworked. Work each side separately. At neck edge of every row dec 1 st twice. Work rem 14 sts until armhole measures 5-1/2 in. (14 cm) = 19 rows. Fasten off. Work other side to correspond.

front

Work same as back until armhole measures 4-1/4 in. (11 cm). Leave the center 15 sts unworked. Work

each side separately. At neck edge of every row, dec 1 st twice. Work rem 14 sts until armhole measures 5-1/4 in. (13.5 cm) = 18 rows. Fasten off. Work the other side to correspond.

sleeves

With crochet hook and blue, ch 43 + ch 2 = first hdc. Work the first hdc in the 4th ch from the hook. Rows 1 and 2: With green, work in hdc = 43 hdc. Row 3: With right side facing, 2 hdc in blue in the first st, 1 hdc in blue, *3 hdc in orange, 3 hdc in blue*, rep * to * 6 times, end last rep with 3 hdc in orange, 1 hdc in blue, 2 hdc in blue in last st. Continue by foll chart. Inc 1 st at each edge of every 4th row 3 times = 51 sts. When piece measures 8-3/4 in. (22 cm), work 1 row sc in blue. Fasten off.

finishing

Block pieces to indicated measurements. Embroider the whiskers with white and the noses in red in satin st. Work 1 row of sc along back shoulders and neck. Work 1 row of red, then work 3 sc in each of the 2 corners. Fasten off. Work 1 row of red sc and 3 sc in each corner of front shoulders and neck. Work 1 row of sc in red as foll: make 2 buttonholes evenly spaced on each shoulder, by skipping 2 sts, ch 2 over skipped sts. Fasten off. With knitting needles and blue, pick up and knit 58 sts from lower edge of back and

work 1-3/4 in. (4.5 cm) in 1/1 ribbing, then work 1 row in red.
Bind off loosely. Work same along
lower edge of front. With knitting
needles and blue, pick up and knit
32 sts from lower edge of each
sleeve and work 1-3/4 in. (4.5 cm)
in 1/1 ribbing. Work 1 row in red.
Bind off loosely. Overlap front
shoulders over back and tack
armhole edge in place. Set in
sleeves. Sew on buttons.

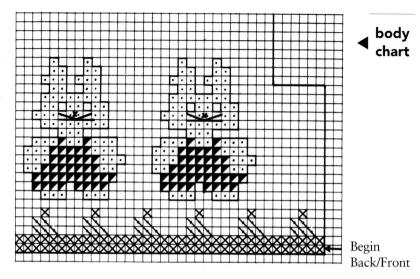

◄ body chart

Begin
Back/Front

sleeve chart ►

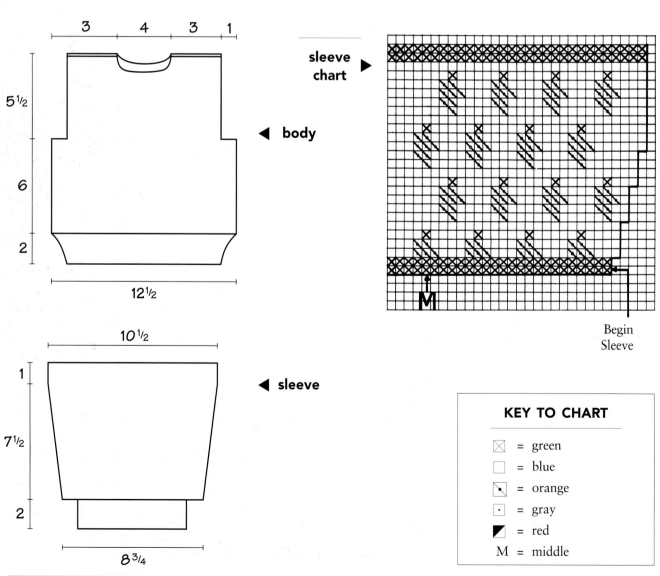

Begin
Sleeve

3   4   3   1

5½

6

2

◄ body

12½

10½

1

7½

2

◄ sleeve

8¾

Ribbon cardigan

This lovely cardigan features fan stitches and pink and white ribbon woven through crocheted eyelets. Mohair makes it extra soft for delicate little ones.

level

Experienced

size

Child's size 1 (2) years, chest 21 (23) in.—53.5 (58.5) cm

finished measurement

Chest: 22 (24) in.—56 (62) cm

Length: 11-1/2 (13-1/2) in.—29 (35) cm

Sleeve seam: 7 (7-1/2) in.—18 (19.5) cm

materials

- Sport weight yarn (approx. 165 yds per 50 g skein) 2 skeins each color light beige, 1 skein each color dark beige, pink, and white, 1 skein light pink mohair yarn

- 5 buttons

- 72 (80) in.—180 (200) cm white ribbon and 22 (24) in.—55 (60) cm pink ribbon

- Crochet hook U.S. size C/2 (Metric size 3) or size needed to obtain gauge
- Knitting needles U.S. size 3 (Metric size 3)

*To save time,
take time to check gauge!*

gauge

20 sts in pat st = 4 in. (10 cm)

stitches

Chain (ch), slip st (sl), single crochet (sc), half double crochet (hdc), double crochet (dc)

1 Deep Sc: Sc, but work around the ch 2 rows below

2 Crossed Deep Dc: Work the first dc around the ch after the sc 2 rows below, then ch 1 and work the 2nd dc around the ch in the front sc 2 rows below.

Bobble: Work 4 dc tog, by working 1 dc until 2 loops rem on hook, then work the 2nd dc until 3 loops rem and so on until 5 loops are on hook. Draw through all loops.

4 Crossed dc: Work 1 dc in the 3rd and 4th dc and work 1 dc in the first and 2nd skipped st.

Pattern st: Work foll the chart, beg as indicated. In the 13th to the 18th rows of the pat st of the pattern, beg with a whole or half fan st. Work whole fan st foll chart 1. For half fan foll chart 2. End row with a whole fan foll chart 2 or half fan st foll chart 2. Work the 6th row of the pat st of crossed dc over 4 sts and work the rem sts at end of row in dc. Beg each row with ch 3 = first dc. On rows of sc, beg with ch 1 = first sc.

Jacquard St: Foll chart in hdc. Beg each row with ch 2. When changing colors, work the last loop of the last st with the color of the next st. Use small bobbins of yarn for each section of color.

1/1 ribbing: Row 1: *K1, p1*. Rep * to * across. Row 2 and all foll rows: Work sts as established in previous row.

Note: See pages 8–18 for detailed instructions on stitches and shapings.

back and sleeves

With crochet hook and light beige, ch 58 (64) + ch 1 (3) = first sc (dc). Continue in pink (light beige). Row 1: In each ch, work 1 sc (dc). Work the first st in the 3rd (5th) ch from the hook = 58 sc (64 dc). Continue by foll chart 1, working the 6th (2nd) row to the 22nd (25th) row = 5 (7) in.—12.5 (17.5) cm from beg. At each edge, inc 30 (33) ch for sleeves as foll: at the end of the last pattern row, ch 30 (33) in white (light beige). For the 2nd sleeve, make a separate ch of 30 (33) sts in white (light beige) and join to end of row. Work 118 (130) sts foll chart 1. For smaller size: work the 23rd to the 28th row, then work the 13th to the 24th rows, then one row of sc in light beige. For larger size: First work the 26th to the 28th rows, then work the 13th to the 28th rows (work the 13th to the 28th rows foll chart 2) and then work the first row of sc in light beige. The sleeve length is now 5-1/4 (5-3/4) in.—13.5 (14.5) cm. Fasten off.

right front with sleeve

With light beige, ch 28 (31) + ch 1 (3) = first sc (dc). Work same as back so that the first row of 28 sc (31 dc) is worked in pink (light beige). Work from the 22nd (25th) row of pat st. At left edge, shape sleeve as on back: ch 30 (33). Continue in pattern beg with row 19 (22) until total height is 8-1/4 (10-3/4) in.—21 (27) cm from beg. At right edge, shape neck. Sl over first 5 (6) sts. At neck edge of foll 3 rows, dec 2 sts. Work rem 47 (52) sts to same height as back. Fasten off.

left front and sleeve

Work same as right front and sleeve, rev shapings. On the 13th row of chart, beg chart 2 (1). Work sleeve by foll chart 2.

finishing

Block pieces to indicated measurements. Sew shoulder and top sleeve seam. With knitting needles and light beige, pick up and knit 59 (63) sts and work 3/4 in. (2 cm) in 1/1 ribbing. Bind off loosely. With knitting needles and light beige, pick up and knit 34 (36) sts along lower edge of each sleeve and work 1-1/4 in. (3 cm) in 1/1 ribbing. Bind off loosely. Work same border along lower edge of body, picking up and knitting 117 (125) sts. With knitting needles and light beige, along right front edge, pick up and knit 73 (87) sts and work in 1/1 ribbing as foll: work 1/4 in. (1 cm), then make 5 buttonholes as foll: right side facing, work 4 (6) sts, *yo, k2 tog, work 14 (17) sts*, rep * to * 3 times, end with yo, k2 tog, work 3 sts. On foll row, work yo's in ribbing. Work until ribbing measures 3/4 in. (2 cm), bind off loosely. Make same border on left front, omitting buttonholes. Thread ribbons through the eyelets of the 9th row and the 21st row of the body and the sleeves. (See photo.) Tack ends of ribbon on wrong side of work. Sew on buttons.

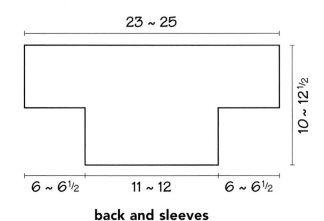

back and sleeves

23 ~ 25

10 ~ 12½

6 ~ 6½   11 ~ 12   6 ~ 6½

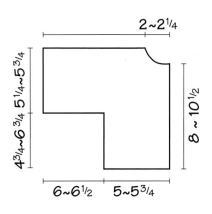

right front and sleeve

2~2¼

4³/₄~6 ³/₄   5¼~5³/₄

8 ~ 10½

6~6½   5~5³/₄

chart 1

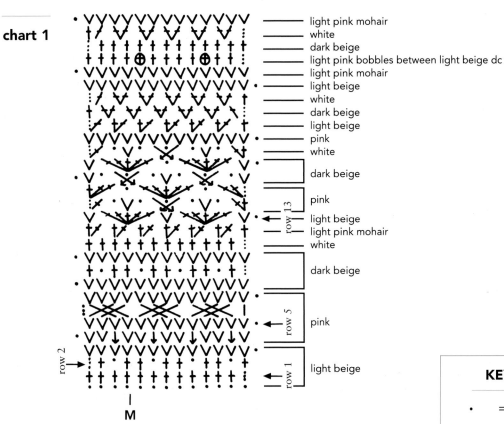

light pink mohair
white
dark beige
light pink bobbles between light beige dc
light pink mohair
light beige
white
dark beige
light beige
pink
white
dark beige
pink
light beige
light pink mohair
white
dark beige
pink
light beige

row 13
row 5
row 1
row 2
M

chart 2

white
dark beige
pink
light beige

row 13

KEY TO CHART

•	=	ch 1
∨	=	1 sc
↓	=	1 deep sc
†	=	1 dc
✗	=	2 crossed deep dc
⋎	=	5 dc in 1 st = fan st
⊕	=	1 bobble
✕✕	=	4 crossed dc
M	=	middle

Matching child's & doll's sweaters

Worsted weight yarn and bold colors combine to make a terrific little girl's sweater. Crochet the matching doll's sweater and let the girl have the pleasure of presenting it to her favorite doll.

level
Intermediate

size
Child's size 2 (3, 4) years

finished measurement
Chest: 28-1/2 (30, 31-1/2) in.—73 (77, 81) cm

Length: 14-1/2 (16, 17) in.—37 (41, 44) cm

Sleeve seam: 9-3/4 (10-1/2, 11-1/4) in.—25 (27, 29) cm

Doll sweater—chest: 14 in. (36 cm); length: 6 in. (15 cm); sleeve seam: 4-1/4 in. (11 cm)

materials
• Mayflower Cotton Helarsgarn - Worsted weight yarn (approx. 86 yds per 50 g skein)

Child's Sweater—3 skeins color green, 2 skeins color blue, 3 skeins color red

• 6 white buttons

Doll's Sweater—1 skein each of above colors

• 4 red buttons

• Crochet hook U.S. size E/4 and F/5 (Metric size 3.5 and 4) or size needed to obtain gauge

To save time, take time to check gauge!

gauge
15 sc and 7-1/2 rows = 4 in. (10 cm)

stitches
Chain (ch), slip st (sl), single crochet (sc), half double crochet (hdc), double crochet (dc)

2 dc worked tog: work the first dc until 2 loops rem on hook, work 2nd dc until 3 loops rem on hook, yo and draw through all loops.

2 sc worked tog: work the first sc until 2 loops rem on hook, work 2nd sc until 3 loops rem on hook, yo and draw through all loops.

Note: See pages 8–18 for detailed instructions on stitches and shapings.

Child's sweater

body
Work the body to the armholes in one piece. Beg each row with ch 3. Pocket linings: With green, ch 18 + ch 3 = first dc. Row 1: 1 dc in the 5th ch from hook, 1 dc in each of the foll 16 ch sts = 18 dc. Work a total of 8 (9, 9) rows. Fasten off.

With crochet hook and green, ch 110 (116, 122) + ch 3 = first dc. Row 1: 1 dc in 5th ch from hook, 1 dc in each rem ch = 110 (116, 122) dc. Work 8 (9, 9) rows. Foll row: Work 9 (10, 11) dc, work across 18 sts of 1 pocket lining, skip 18 dc of row, work 56 (60, 64) dc, work 18 dc of 2nd pocket lining, skip 18 sts, work last 9 (10, 11) dc = 110 (116, 122) dc. Work a total of 16 (18, 20) rows. Fasten off. Work 1 row in red in hdc. Fasten off.

Now work in separate sections in blue. For right front, work over first 25 (26, 27) dc for 10 (11, 12) rows in dc. Foll row: Leave 8 sts unworked at neck edge, work 15 (16, 17) dc and then work last 2 dc tog at neck edge = 16 (17, 18) dc. Fasten off. Make left front by rev shapings. Leave 8 sts unworked for armholes and work over center 44 (48, 52) dc for back for 11 (12, 13) rows. Fasten off.

sleeves
With crochet hook and red, ch 32 (35, 37) + ch 3 = first dc. Row 1: 1 dc in 5th ch from hook, 1 dc in each rem ch = 32 (35, 37) dc. Work for 23 (24, 26) rows. At the same time, inc at each edge of every 6th row, then inc 1 st at each edge of every 2nd row 7 times. (At beg of row, ch 5 instead of ch 3, 1 dc in the 5th ch from hook, 1 dc in each of the foll dc, at end of row, work 1 tr under the last worked dc = 46 (49, 51) dc.) Fasten off.

finishing
Block pieces to indicated measurements. Sew shoulder seams. With blue, work 38 (40, 42) dc along neck edges, leaving 3 sts unworked at each edge. Work 1 dc in each st, 2 dc in each corner and 2 dc in each dc row. Fasten off. Along lower edge, front edges, and collar edges, work 1 row of sc in matching colors. Work along lower edge of body first, work 2 sc per row along front edges and 3 sc in corners. Work 1 row of sc in red as foll: in corner, 3 sc, work in the corner of the collar, work 2 sc tog and make 6 buttonholes along right front edge between collar and top of pocket as foll: for each buttonhole, ch 5, skip 2. Fasten off. With red, work 1 row of sc along top of pockets. Fasten off. Sew pockets in place. Along lower edges of sleeves, work 1 row of sc with green and 1 row with blue. Fasten off. Sew sleeve seams, rev seam for cuffs. Set in sleeves. Sew on buttons.

Doll's sweater

body

Worked in 1 piece to armholes. Beg each row with ch 3 = first dc.

pocket linings

With green, ch 8 + ch 3 = first dc. Row 1: 1 dc in the 5th ch from hook, 1 dc in each of the foll 6 ch = 8 dc. Work 3 rows of dc and fasten off.

body

With crochet hook and green, ch 60 + ch 3 = first dc. Row 1: 1 dc in 5th ch from hook, 1 dc in each rem ch = 60 dc. Rows 2-4: Dc. Row 5: Work 5 dc, work across 8 dc of pocket lining, skip 8 dc of row, work 34 dc, work 8 dc of 2nd pocket lining, skip 8 dc of row, work rem 5 dc. Work 2 rows of dc in green. Work 1 row of sc in red. Now work in separate parts in blue. Over right front, work 6 rows of dc over first 11 sts. Fasten off. Work left front over the last 11 sts for 6 rows. Work 7 sts unworked at each edge of center sts and work 24 sts for back. Work 6 rows of dc. Fasten off.

sleeves

With crochet hook and red, ch 24 + ch 3 = first dc. Row 1: 1 dc in the 5th ch from the hook, 1 dc in each of the foll 22 ch sts = 24 dc. Work in dc for 10 rows. Inc 1 st at each edge of 5th and 7th rows as foll: at beg of row, ch 5 instead of ch 3, 1 dc in the 5th ch from the hook, 1 dc in each of the foll dc. At end of row, work 1 tr under the last dc. Fasten off.

finishing

Block pieces to indicated measurements. Sew shoulder seams over 6 sts. With blue, work 30 dc along neck edge. Along lower edge, front edges, and collar edges, work 1 row of sc in matching colors. Fasten off. Work along lower edge of body first, work 2 sc per row along front edges and 3 sc in corners. Work 1 row of sc in red as foll: in corner, 3 sc, work in the corner of the collar, work 2 sc tog and make 4 buttonholes along right front edge between collar and top of pocket as foll: for each buttonhole, ch 5, skip 3. Fasten off. With red, work 1 row of sc along top of pockets. Fasten off. Sew pockets in place. Along lower edges of sleeves, work 1 row of sc with green and 1 row with blue. Sew on buttons.

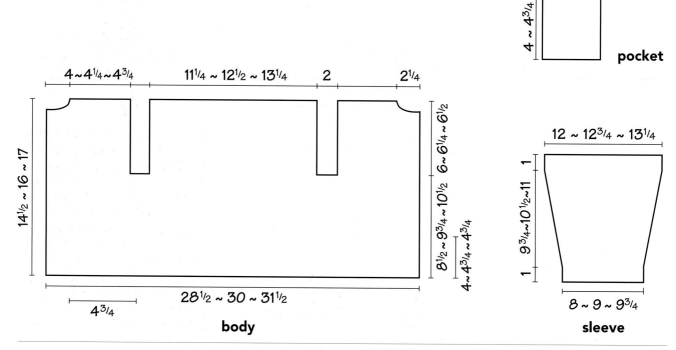

pocket

body

sleeve

Striped sweater & hat

For that special little beachcomber in your life, here's a boldly striped sweater and matching hat. Jacquard and shrimp stitches give the set an appealing texture.

level

Intermediate

size

Child's size 2 (4, 5) years, chest 21 (23, 25) in.—53 (58, 63) cm

finished measurement

Chest: 24 (26, 28) in.—62 (67, 72) cm

Length: 12-1/2 (14-1/2, 16-1/2) in.—32 (37, 42) cm

Sleeve seam: 2 in. (5 cm)

materials

- Mayflower Cotton 8 - Sport weight yarn (approx. 186 yds per 50 g skein) 2 (2, 3) skeins each color blue and white
- 4 buttons
- Elastic
- Crochet hook U.S. size B/1 (Metric size 2.5) or size needed to obtain gauge
- Knitting needles U.S. size 4 (Metric size 3.5)

To save time, take time to check gauge!

gauge

11 motifs in background and 24 rows = 4 in. (10 cm)

stitches

Chain (ch), slip st (sl), single crochet (sc), half double crochet (hdc)

Jacquard St: Foll chart in hdc. Beg each row with ch 2. When changing colors, work the last loop of the last st with the color of the next st.

Shrimp St: Worked like sc, but worked left to right instead of right to left.

Background pattern: Row 1: Ch 1, *In 1 st: 1 sc, ch 1, 1 sc; skip 1 st*, rep * to *. Row 2 and all foll rows: Ch 1, *1 sc, ch 1, 1 sc in the first sc in the motif (1 motif = 1 sc, ch 1, 1 sc)*, rep * to *, end with 1 sc in the turning ch.

Stripes: *2 rows blue, 4 rows white, 4 rows blue, 2 rows white*, rep * to *.

1/1 ribbing: Row 1: *K1, p1*. Rep * to * across. Row 2 and all foll rows: Work sts as established in previous row.

Note: See pages 8–18 for detailed instructions on stitches and shapings.

front

With knitting needles and white, cast on 68 (74, 80) sts and work 1-1/2 in. (4 cm) in 1/1 ribbing. Bind off, putting last loop on crochet hook. With crochet hook and white, work 1 st in each knitted st and work first row of background st = 34 (37, 40) motifs. Work the last loop in blue. Continue in background st (row 2) and stripes and work the last loop of one color with a strand of the foll color. Work until piece measures 7

(8-3/4, 10-1/4) in.—18 (22, 26) cm. On the foll row, leave 4 motifs unworked at each edge. Work rem 26 (29, 32) motifs until armhole measures 5-1/4 (5-1/2, 6) in.—13 (14, 15) cm. Leave the center 8 (9, 10) motifs unworked. Work each shoulder separately. At each neck edge of foll 2 rows, leave 1/2 motif unworked. Work rem 8 (9, 10) motifs on each shoulder until armhole measures 7-1/2 (8, 8-3/4) in.—19 (20, 22) cm. On the foll row, make 2 buttonholes as foll: beg at neck edge, work 1 motif, ch 3, skip 1 motif, work 3 motifs, ch 3 and skip 1 motif and work to end of row. On foll row, work 1 motif in the center ch. Fasten off. Work other side to correspond.

back

Work same as front until armhole measures 9 (10, 10) in.—3-1/2 (4, 4) cm. End with 1 row of white. Fasten off.

sleeves

With knitting needles and white, cast on 62 (66, 70) sts and work 3/4 in. (2 cm) in 1/1 ribbing. Bind off. With crochet hook and white, work first row of background st in the loops of the last row of 1/1 ribbing. Work the last loop of the last st with blue. Work over 31 (33, 35) motifs as foll: 4 rows blue, 2 rows white, 2 rows blue, 4 rows white, then work in blue until sleeve measures 3-1/2 in. (9 cm). Fasten off.

finishing

Block pieces to indicated measurements. With crochet hook and white, work 1 row of sc along back neck and shoulder band edges and along the upper front edges, then work first row of background pat. Overlap back shoulder bands 1/4 in. (1 cm) over the front edges and tack in place. Sew sleeves to armholes, sewing top 1-1/2 in. (4 cm) of sleeve to armhole. Sew side and sleeve seams. Sew on buttons.

at

Hat width: 18-1/2 in. (46 cm)

With crochet hook and blue, ch 4. Sl st to join in ring. Continue in blue in rounds of hdc. Beg each round with ch 2 and end round with sl st in the 2nd ch from the beg of round. Round 1: 10 hdc in ring. Round 2: Hdc, working 2 hdc in every st = 20 hdc. Round 3: Hdc with 2 hdc in every 2nd st = 30 hdc. Round 4: Hdc with 2 hdc in every 3rd st = 40 hdc. Round 5: Hdc with 2 hdc in every 4th st = 50 hdc. Round 6: Hdc with 2 hdc in every 5th st = 60 hdc. Round 7: Hdc with 2 hdc with every 6th st = 70 hdc. Work the last loop of the last st in white

and continue in background st. Sl st in the turning ch of every round. Work 4 rounds white, 4 rounds blue, 2 rounds white, 2 rounds blue, 4 rounds white and end in blue. At the same time, work as foll: Rounds 8 and 9: Work 35 motifs. Round 10: Inc 5 motifs evenly spaced around = 40 motifs. Round 11: 40 motifs and make the last loop in blue. Round 12: Inc 4 motifs evenly spaced around. Round 13: 44 motifs. Rounds 14 and 15: 44 motifs, work the last loop of the last st in white. Rounds 16 and 17: 44 motifs, work the last loop in blue. Rounds 18 and 19: 44 motifs, make the last loop in white. Round 20: At center back, at each edge of the slipped st, inc a total of 5 motifs = 49 motifs. Rounds 21–23: 49 motifs and work the last loop in blue. Work 4 rounds of blue. Beg at center back, work 12 motifs, turn, work 24 motifs. Turn. Sl over 6 motifs and work 12 motifs. Turn. Sl over 6 motifs and work 6 motifs. Fasten off in blue. Join white to

beg at beg of round, work 1 round of 49 motifs. Without turning, work 1 hdc in every sc = 98 hdc. Fasten off.

ill

With blue, over the center 44 hdc, work 44 sc. Foll row: Ch 2, work 2 sc tog, work to last 2 sc, work 2 sc tog. Foll row: Ch 2, work 2 sc tog, work to last 3 sc, work 2 sc tog, 1 hdc. Rep the last row until 14 sc rem. Fasten off. Join blue yarn at beg of bill and work 1 row of shrimp st (like sc, but work left to right instead of right to left). Work the last loop of the last st in white and work 1 row of shrimp st in white around the lower edge of hat. Fasten off.

finishing

Starch the bill. Sew a piece of elastic to the inside back of the hat.

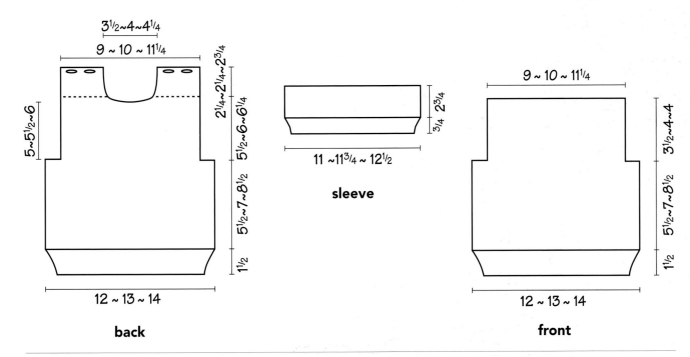

back

sleeve

front

Yellow sweater

This sunny yellow top, with its easy fit boat neck, and cool, waffle pattern, is a real child-pleaser.

level

Intermediate

size

Child's size 2 (4, 6) years

finished measurement

Chest: 26 (28, 30) in.—66 (71, 76) cm

Length: 12-1/2 (13-1/4, 14) in.—32 (34, 36) cm

Sleeve seam: 1-3/4 (2, 2-1/2) in.—4.5 (5.5, 6.5) cm

materials

• Mayflower Cotton 8 - Sport weight yarn (approx. 186 yds per 50 g skein) 4 (4, 5) skeins color yellow

• Crochet hook U.S. size B/1 (Metric size 2.5) or size needed to obtain gauge

To save time, take time to check gauge!

gauge

27 sts and 19 rows = 4 in. (10 cm)

stitches

Chain (ch), slip st (sl), single crochet (sc), double crochet (dc)

Pattern St: Worked on a chain with a multiple of 3 + 2 + ch 2 to turn. Row 1: 1 dc in the 5th ch from the hook, *ch 1, skip 1 ch, 2 dc*, rep * to *. Row 2: Ch 1 to turn = first sc, 1 sc in the foll dc, *1 sc in ch and 1 sc in each dc*, rep * to *. Row 3: Ch 3, 1 dc in the foll sc, *ch 1, skip 1 sc, 1 dc in the foll 2 sc*, rep * to *. Always rep rows 2 and 3.

Note: See pages 8–18 for detailed instructions on stitches and shapings.

back

Ch 92 (98, 104) + ch 3 = first st. Work in pat st until piece measures 6-3/4 (7, 7-1/4) in.—17 (18, 19) cm from beg. Shape sleeves. Ch 12 (15, 18) at end of next 2 rows and continue in pat st. When piece measures 6 (6-1/4, 6-1/2) in.—15 (16, 17) cm from beg of armhole, fasten off.

front

Work same as back.

finishing

Block pieces to indicated measurements. Sew shoulder seams leaving center 4 (4-1/4, 4-3/4) in.—10 (11, 12) cm open for neck. Sew side and sleeve seams.

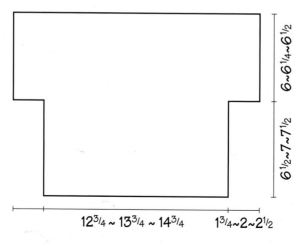

6~6¹⁄₄~6¹⁄₂

6¹⁄₂~7~7¹⁄₂

12³⁄₄ ~ 13³⁄₄ ~ 14³⁄₄   1³⁄₄~2~2¹⁄₂

back – front

Starfish top

Here's a summer gift that will bring a sunny smile to a child's face: a pair of crocheted starfish sewn onto a filet crochet top.

level

Intermediate

size

Child's size 18 months/2 years, chest 21 in.—(52.5 cm)

finished measurement

Chest: 20-1/4 in. (52 cm)

Length: 6 in. (15 cm)

materials

- Mayflower Cotton 8 - Sport weight cotton yarn (approx. 186 yds per 50 g skein) 2 skeins color dark yellow
- Crochet hook U.S. size C/2 (Metric size 2.5) or size needed to obtain gauge

*To save time,
take time to check gauge!*

gauge

10 squares and 10 rows = 4 in. (10 cm)

stitches

Chain (ch), slip st (sl), single crochet (sc), half double crochet (hdc), double crochet (dc), treble (tr)

Filet crochet: 1 open square = 1 dc, ch 2, skip 2, 1 dc. 1 filled square = 4 dc. The last dc of the previous square is the first dc of the foll square. Ch 3 to turn when the first square is an open square.

Note: See pages 8–18 for detailed instructions on stitches and shapings.

front

Worked from side to side. With crochet hook, ch 46 + ch 3 = first dc, 1 dc in the 5th ch from the hook, 2 dc = 1 filled square, 13 open squares, 1 filled square. Row 2: 2 filled squares, 12 open squares, 1 filled square. Row 3: 1 filled square, 13 open squares, 1 filled square. Always rep the 2nd to the 3rd row until you have 52 rows. Sew the last row to the first row.

shoulder bands

Ch 7, 1 dc in the 5th ch from the hook, 2 dc; work a total of 23 rows of 4 dc. Sew shoulder bands to the 7th square from the side seam. Work as foll: *1 sc in the dc, 1 picot = ch 3, 1 sc in the 3rd ch from the hook*, rep * to *.

starfish

Large starfish: ch 5, sl st to join in ring. Row 1: *2 dc in the ring, ch 1*, rep * to * 5 times. Row 2: Sl st to the ch, *1 sc in ch, 1 sc, ch 10, sl st in 3rd ch from hook, sl st, 3 sc, 3 hdc, 3 dc, 3 tr*, rep * to * 4 times. Fasten off. Small starfish: Ch 5, sl st to join in ring. Row 1: 10 sc in ring, sl st to join in ring. Row 2: *1 sc, ch 10, sl st in the 3rd ch from hook, sl st, 2 sc, 2 hdc, 2 dc, skip 1 sc*, rep * to * 4 times. Fasten off. Sew starfish to front. See photo.

Baby t-shirt

This American flag-colored T-shirt is perfect for Fourth of July weather, with its filet openwork and crisp colors. It's so easy to make, you'll have time for an extra swim!

level
Intermediate

size
Baby's size 3 (6, 12) months

finished measurement
Chest: 22 (23, 25) in.—55 (59, 63) cm

Length: 10 (11, 12) in.—26 (28.5, 30.5) cm

Sleeve seam: 1-1/4 in. (3 cm)

materials
- Mayflower Cotton 8 - Sport weight yarn (approx. 186 yds per 50 g skein) 1 skein each color white, blue, and red
- 4 white buttons
- Crochet hook U.S. size B/1 (Metric size 2.5) or size needed to obtain gauge

To save time, take time to check gauge!

gauge
14-1/2 squares and 13 rows = 4 in. (10 cm)

stitches
Chain (ch), single crochet (sc), double crochet (dc)

Filet St: Work by foll chart. One open square is 1 dc, ch 1, skip 1, 1 dc. Ch 4 is the first st of open square = the first dc.

Note: See pages 8–18 for detailed instructions on stitches and shapings.

back
With blue, ch 81 (87, 93) + ch 4 to turn = first open square. Row 1: 1 dc in the 7th ch from the hook, *ch 1, skip 1 ch, 1 dc*, rep * to * = 40 (43, 46) squares. Work 11 (12, 13) rows in blue, 11 (12, 13) rows in white and 11 (12, 13) rows in red. Complete in red. Leave the center 14 (15, 16) squares unworked for neck. Work 2 rows of 14 (15, 16) squares over each shoulder. Fasten off.

front
Work same as back, but work 1 row instead of 2 rows on each shoulder.

finishing
Block pieces to indicated measurements. Work 1 row of sc along the shoulder and neck edge of both pieces in red. Fasten off. Place the last row of open squares of front over the last row of back and tack in place. For sleeves, with red, work 4 rows of open squares over the top 14 (15, 16) rows of body = 28 (30, 32) open squares. Fasten off. Sew side and sleeve seams in matching colors. With red, work 1 row of sc around sleeve ends. Fasten off. With blue, work 1 row of sc around lower edge of body. Fasten off. Sew buttons to shoulders, using open squares as buttonholes.

Heart top

This heart-decorated top uses filet crochet to achieve a lacelike effect sure to win her heart.

level

Intermediate

size

Child's size 10/12 years, chest 28–30 in.—(71.5, 75 cm)

finished measurement

Chest: 36 in. (92 cm)

Length: 19 in. (48 cm)

materials

- Mayflower Cotton 8 - Sport weight cotton yarn (approx. 186 yds per 50 g skein) 5 skeins color white
- Crochet hook U.S. size C/2 (Metric size 2.5) or size needed to obtain gauge
- Knitting needles U.S. size 2 (Metric size 2)

To save time, take time to check gauge!

gauge

13-1/2 squares and 12-1/2 rows = 4 in. (10 cm)

stitches

Chain (ch), slip st (sl), single crochet (sc), double crochet (dc)

Filet crochet: work hearts foll the chart: 1 open square = 1 dc, ch 1, skip 1, 1 dc. 1 filled square = 3 dc. The last dc of the previous square is the first dc of the foll square. Ch 4 to turn when the first square is an open square.

1/1 ribbing: Row 1: *K1, p1*. Rep * to * across. Row 2 and all foll rows: Work sts as established in previous row.

Note: See pages 8–18 for detailed instructions on stitches and shapings.

body

Worked in 1 piece, beg at the lower edge of the front. With crochet hook, ch 127 + ch 4 to turn. Row 1: Work the first dc in the 7th ch from the hook = first open square, continue by working 62 more open squares. Work over these 63 open squares until piece measures 11 in. (28 cm). Foll row: For the sleeves, make 2 separate 16 ch st pieces and join to each edge of the last row. Ch 4, work first dc in the 7th ch from the hook. Work 7 open squares, 63 open squares of the body, 8 open squares on the 2nd chain = 79 squares. Work 6 rows of open squares, work 7 rows of hearts foll the chart, 3 rows of open squares. Leave the center 29 squares unworked and work each side separately for 8 rows = 2-1/2 in. (6.5 cm) 25 open squares. Join the 2 sides by chaining 57 sts between them. Work 21 rows of open squares. The sleeve height is 14-1/4 in. (36 cm). Leave 8 squares unworked at each edges and work rem 63 squares of back until side seams measures 11 in. (28 cm). Fasten off.

finishing

Block pieces to indicated measurements. With knitting needles, pick up and knit 1 st from every st along lower edge of back and front and work 3/4 in. (2 cm) in 1/1 ribbing. Bind off. Sew side and sleeve seams. Work 1 row of sc along neck and sleeve edges. Fasten off.

front – back

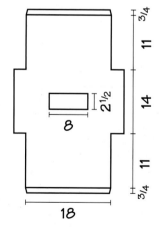

center front

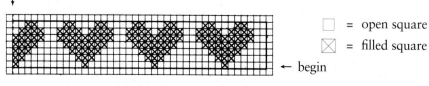

□ = open square

⊠ = filled square

← begin

Red heart top

This sweetheart cotton top makes a lovely gift. She'll love the spaghetti straps that cross in the back.

level

Intermediate

size

Child's size 10/12 years, chest 28–30 in.—(71.5-75 cm)

finished measurement

Chest: 32-3/4 in. (82 cm)

Length: 13-1/2 in. (34 cm)

materials

• Mayflower Cotton 8 - Sport weight cotton yarn (approx. 186 yds per 50 g skein) 4 skeins color red

• Crochet hook U.S. size B/1 (Metric size 2) or size needed to obtain gauge

• Knitting needles U.S. size 2 (Metric size 2)

To save time, take time to check gauge!

gauge

12-1/2 squares and 10 rows = 4 in. (10 cm)

stitches

Chain (ch), slip st (sl), single crochet (sc), double crochet (dc)

Filet crochet: Work heart foll the chart: 1 open square = 1 dc, ch 1, skip 1, 1 dc. 1 filled square = 3 dc. The last dc of the previous square is the first dc of the foll square. Ch 4 to turn when the first square is an open square.

1/1 ribbing: Row 1: *K1, p1*. Rep * to * across. Row 2 and all foll rows: Work sts as established in previous row.

Note: See pages 8–18 for detailed instructions on stitches and shapings.

front

With crochet hook, ch 103 + ch 4 to turn. Row 1: Work the first dc in the 7th ch from the hook = first open square, continue by working 50 more open squares = 51 open squares. Continue by foll chart. Fasten off.

back

Ch 103 + ch 4 = first open square. Work 30 rows over 51 open squares.

finishing

Block pieces to indicated measurements. With knitting needles, pick up and knit 88 sts along lower edge of back and front and work 1-1/2 in. (4 cm) in 1/1 ribbing. Bind off. Sew side seams. Work 2 rows of sc along top edges. Fasten off. For shoulder straps, make 2 chains 18 in. (45 cm) long and work 1 row of sc along chain. Join straps above the 14th square from each side seam and cross at back.

← begin

☐ = open square

⊠ = filled square

Blue top

The interplay of closed and open squares creates a lovely patchwork-quilt effect, and the slight off-the-shoulder neckline is very flattering.

level

Intermediate

size

Woman's size X-Small (Small, Medium, Large), chest 30-1/2 (31- 1/2, 32) in.—78 (80, 82.5) cm.

finished measurement

Chest: 35 (38-1/4, 40) in.—90 (98, 103) cm

Length: 19 (20-1/4, 21) in.—48 (52, 53) cm

Sleeve seam: 4-1/2 (5-1/4, 5-1/4) in.—11.5 (13.5, 13.5) cm

materials

• Mayflower Cotton 8 - Sport weight yarn (approx. 186 yds per 50 g skein) 6 (7, 7) skeins blue

• Crochet hook U.S. size B/1 (Metric size 2.5) or size needed to obtain gauge

• Knitting needles U.S. size 2 (Metric size 2)

To save time, take time to check gauge!

gauge

13-1/2 squares and 10-1/2 rows = 4 in. (10 cm)

stitches

Chain (ch), single crochet (sc), half double crochet (hdc)

Filet St: Work by foll chart. One open square equals 1 dc, ch 1, skip 1, 1 dc; 1 filled square is 3 dc. The last dc of the previous square is the first dc of the foll square. Ch 3 or 4 is the first st of open square. Ch 4 = the first dc, ch 3 = first sc.

1/1 ribbing: Row 1: *K1, p1*. Rep * to * across. Row 2 and all foll rows: Work sts as established in previous row.

Note: See pages 8–18 for detailed instructions on stitches and shapings.

back

With crochet hook, ch 123 (135, 143) + ch 4 to turn = first st. Row 1: 1 dc in the 7th ch from the hook, *ch 1, skip 1 ch, 1 dc*, rep * to* = 61 (67, 71) squares. Work 2 (1, 2) rows of open squares. Foll row: 4 (1, 3) open squares, *5 filled squares, 7 open squares*, rep * to * 4 (5, 5) times, 5 filled squares, 4 (1, 3) open squares = first row of block motif. Continue by centering chart. When back measures 15 (17, 17-1/4) in.— 37.5 (42.5, 43) cm from beg = 39 (44, 45) rows, leave the center 29 (33, 35) squares unworked. Work 5 rows on 16 (17, 18) squares on each shoulder = 16-3/4 (18-3/4, 19) in.—42 (47, 47.5) cm from beg. Fasten off.

front

Work same as back.

sleeves

With crochet hook, ch 87 (95, 99), ch 4 = first open square. Row 1: *ch 1, skip 1 ch, 1 dc*, rep * to* = 43 (47, 49) open squares. Work 0 (1, 1) row of open squares. Foll row: 1 (3, 4) open squares, *5 filled squares, 7 open squares*, rep * to* 3 times, 5 filled squares, 1 (3, 4) open squares = first row of chart. Continue by centering chart = 12 (14, 14) rows. At the same time, at each edge of every 5 (6, 6) rows, inc 1 square (through the edge dc, ch 1 and work 1 extra dc). Fasten off.

finishing

Block pieces to indicated measurements. With knitting needles, pick up 94 (98, 100) sts and work 2-1/2 (2, 2-1/2) in.—6 (5, 6) cm in 1/1 ribbing. Bind off loosely. Sew shoulder seams. Sew sleeves to side seams, matching center of sleeve to shoulder seams. Sew side and sleeve seams. With crochet hook, work 1 row of sc around neck and sleeve ends. Fasten off.

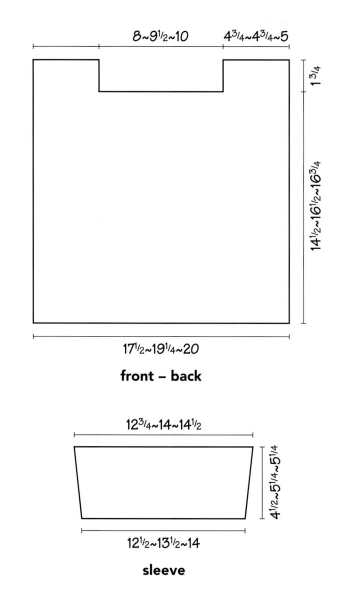

front – back

sleeve

KEY TO CHART

☐ = open square

☒ = filled square

M = center

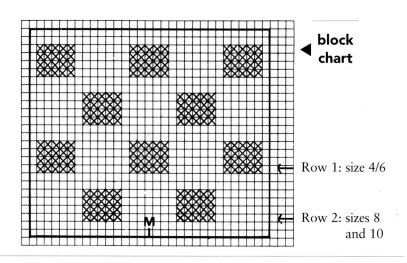

block chart

Row 1: size 4/6

Row 2: sizes 8 and 10

Nursery favorites

Toy train

These colorful trains will surely fuel the imagination of the youngest conductor. The crocheted pieces are sewn around soft foam rubber blocks.

level
Intermediate

finished measurement
Width: 7 in. (18 cm); height: 6 in. (15 cm); depth: 3-1/4 in. (8 cm)—measurements of each locomotive and wagon

materials
- Mayflower Cotton Helarsgarn - Worsted weight cotton yarn (approx. 86 yds per 50 g skein) 1 skein each color red, yellow, blue, green, and black
- Small amount of Mayflower Cotton 8 - Sport weight cotton yarn in black
- 8 wooden wheels
- 8 thin dowels to fit
- 3 pieces of wood 7 x 3-1/4 in. (18 x 8 cm)
- 16 small brads
- Fiberfill
- 3 foam rubber blocks 3-1/4 in. (8 cm) thick, 7 in. (18 cm) long, and 6 in. (15 cm) high
- Crochet hook U.S. size H/8 (Metric size 5) or size needed to obtain gauge

To save time, take time to check gauge!

gauge
13 sc and 15 rows = 4 in. (10 cm)

stitches
Chain (ch), slip st (sl), single crochet (sc)

Note: See pages 8–18 for detailed instructions on stitches and shapings.

directions
Work each side in Mayflower Helarsgarn in desired colors. Sew the pieces together with Mayflower Cotton 8.

Wagon

With crochet hook and desired color, make a chain 7 in. (18 cm) long. Work in sc until piece measures 6 in. (15 cm) high. Fasten off. Make 2 sides. Make back and front sections by making a chain 3-1/4 in. (8 cm) wide. Work in sc until piece measures 6 in. (15 cm) high. Fasten off. For the top and bottom, make a chain 3-1/4 in. (8 cm) wide. Work in sc until piece measures 7 in. (18 cm) high. Fasten off. Make these pieces for each wagon. For each wagon, make 2 pieces in each color.

ℒocomotive

Work bottom and back pieces in the same manner as the wagon. For the 2 sides, make a chain 3-1/2 in. (9 cm) wide and work in sc until piece measures 6 in. (15 cm) high. Fasten off. For the 2 short sides, make a chain 3-1/2 in. (9 cm) wide and work until piece measures 3 in. (7 cm) high. Fasten off. For the two top rectangles, make a chain 3-1/4 in. (8 cm) wide and work until piece measures 3-1/2 in. (9 cm) high. Fasten off. Make the 2 front rectangles by making a chain 3-1/4 in. (8 cm) wide and work until piece measures 3 in. (7.5 cm) high. Fasten off.

𝒮mokestack

Ch 6 and sl st to join in ring. Round 1: 8 sc in the ring. Sl st to join each round and ch 1 = first sc. Round 2: Ch 1 = first sc, *2 sc in the foll sc, 1 sc in each of the foll sc*, rep * to * = 12 sc. Round 3: Ch 1 = first sc, 2 sc in each of the foll sc, end with 1 sc in the first st = 24 sc. Round 4: Ch 1 = first sc, work 2 sc tog = 12 sc. Round 5: Ch 1 = first sc, *work 2 sc tog, 1 sc in the foll sc*, rep * to * = 8 sc. Rounds 6 to 11: Work 1 sc in each sc. Fasten off.

finishing

Embroider with Mayflower Cotton 8 on the sides of each wagon, separating rows of stem st with 1 sc. See photo. On fronts and backs, make smaller rows of stem st. Sew the top, sides, front, and back around the foam rubber blocks. Use Helarsgarn and sew in decorative zigzag st around seams. See photo. For the underside of each wagon, insert dowel and glue into wheels. With crimpers and brads, evenly space 3 sets of wheels to the wood pieces. Sew the bottom of the block in place with the wood piece inside the crocheted pieces and the wheels at the sides. Make the locomotive in the same manner, but instead of 3 sets of wheels, put one set of wheels under the front and back of the locomotive. Sew the pieces tog same as the wagon, using photo as a guide. Sew on the smokestack. Make a chain in black about 12 in. (30 cm) long and sew to front of locomotive. Make chains 2-1/2 in. (6 cm) long and join pieces tog.

Play ball!

Foam-filled balls are fun to hold and toss, and the lively patterns will captivate baby's attention over and over again.

level

Intermediate

materials

- Mayflower Cotton 8 - Sport weight yarn (approx. 186 yds per 50 g skein) 1 skein each color pink, white, light blue, and red
- 6 foam balls 2-3/4 in. (7 cm) in diameter
- Steel crochet hook U.S. size 5 (Metric size 1.5) or size needed to obtain gauge

To save time, take time to check gauge!

gauge

36-1/2 sts and 33-1/2 rows = 4 in. (10 cm)

stitches

Chain (ch), slip st (sl), single crochet (sc)

Note: See pages 8–18 for detailed instructions on stitches and shapings.

directions

Ch 2 = first sc. End each round with 1 sl st in the first st. When changing colors, work the last loop of the last st with the color of the next st. Carry the unused yarn across wrong side of work. The ball is made of two halves which are precisely the same. Work all balls same as the light blue striped ball, adjusting colors as described.

Light blue striped ball

With crochet hook and light blue, ch 6 and sl st to join in ring. Round 1: 9 sc in ring. Round 2: Sc, inc 4 sc evenly spaced around = 13 sc. Round 3: sc, inc 5 sc evenly spaced around = 18 sc. Round 4: Sc, working 2 sc in every 2nd sc = 27 sc. Round 5: With white, sc, working 2 sc in every 3rd sc = 36 sc. Round 6: With white, sc, working 2 sc in every 4th sc = 45 sc. Round 7: With light blue, sc. Round 8: With light blue, sc, working 2 sc in every 5th sc = 54 sc. Round 9: With white, sc. Round 10: With white, sc, working 2 sc in every 6th sc = 63 sc. Round 11: With light blue, sc. Round 12: With light blue, sc, working 2 sc in every 7th sc = 72 sc. Rounds 13 and 14: With white, sc. Rounds 15 and 16: With light blue, sc. Rounds 17 and 18: With white, sc. Fasten off. Embroider 9 lines with a double strand of light blue over the 2 white rows. Make 2 halves and insert foam ball. Sew tog with light blue yarn. See photo.

Pink & white striped ball

Work in sts as above. Beg with white. Rounds 1–3: White. Round 4: Pink. Round 5: White. Round 6: Pink. Rounds 7–10: White. Round 11: Pink. Round 12: White. Round 13: Pink. Rounds 14–17: White. Round 18: Pink. Fasten off. Embroider with a double strand of pink over the white row between the 2 pink rows after every 3rd st. See photo. Sew the 2 halves tog with a strand of white over the white sts and pink over the pink sts.

Pink ball with white band

Work in sts as above. Beg with white. Rounds 1–3: White. Round 4: Alternately work 2 sts in white, 1 st in pink. Rounds 5–18: Work 2 white sts above the 2 white sts of round 3. Work the sts between in pink. Sew the 2 halves tog with a strand of pink over the pink sts and white over the white sts.

White ball with red petals

Work same as the pink ball with white band to round 12, but work in red instead of pink. Round 13: 3 sc in white, *4 sc in red, 4 sc in white*, rep * to *, end with 4 sc in red, 1 sc in white. Round 14: 4 sc in white, *2 sc in red, 6 sc in white*, rep * to *, end with 2 sc in red, 2 sc in white. Rounds 15–18: Sc in white. Fasten off. Sew the 2 halves tog with white yarn.

White ball with light blue bands

The incs worked after the 3rd round should be worked in white. Beg with light blue. Rounds 1–4: Sc in light blue. Round 5: *3 sc in light blue, 1 sc in white*, rep * to *. Work the foll rounds, working 3 sts in light blue above the 3 sts in light blue of the previous rounds and the rem sts in white. Fasten off. Sew the 2 halves tog with white yarn over the white sts and blue yarn over the blue sts.

Red ball with white petals

Work same as white ball with red petals, but rev colors.

Baby blanket

Pastel-colored trains and wagons embroidered over Tunisian-style squares are certain to transport some lucky baby off to dreamland.

level

Intermediate

finished measurement

24 x 30 in. (60 x 77 cm)

materials

- Worsted weight yarn (approx. 100 yds per 50 g skein) 8 skeins color ecru
- Tapestry wool, used double, in the following colors: light pink, rose, gold, and blue
- Tapestry wool, using 7 strands together, color light blue.
- Afghan crochet hook U.S. size J/10 (Metric size 6)
- Crochet hook U.S. size F/5 (Metric size 4) or size needed to obtain gauge

To save time, take time to check gauge!

gauge

15 sts and 14 rows = 4 in. (10 cm)

stitches

Chain (ch), single crochet (sc)

Tunisian st: Each row is worked back and forth, beg on a chain. Row 1: Right side of work: yo, draw 1 loop through the 2nd ch from hook, draw 1 loop through every foll loop. All loops stay on the hook. Yo, draw through 1 loop, *yo, draw through 2 loops*, rep * to * so that 1 st rem on hook. Row 2: Yo, draw through 1 loop, *yo, draw through 2 loops*, rep * to * so that 1 st rem on hook. Row 3: *Insert hook through the vertical loop of the foll st and draw through 1 loop*, rep * to * so that all loops rem on the hook. Row 4: Yo, draw through 1 loop, *yo, draw through 2 loops rep * to* until 1 loop remains o hook. Always rep rows 3 and 4 First and last sts are border sts.

Note: See pages 8–18 for detailed instructions on stitches and shapings.

directions

Make 25 squares in Tunisian stitch. With afghan hook and ecru, ch 19 and work in Tunisian stitch = 18 sts. Work 21 rows. After the last row, work 1 row of sc. Fasten off.

finishing

Block pieces to indicated measurements. Embroider 12 squares in locomotive or wagon motif. Beg embroidery at lower right corner in the 3rd st of the 6th row. See photo. Lay the squares 5 high and 5 wide, alternating embroidered and unembroidered squares. With light blue in zigzag stitch, sew the squares together vertically first, then horizontally. With ecru, work 1 row of sc around the outside blanket edge, with 1 sc in each st and 2 sc in each corner. Fasten off.

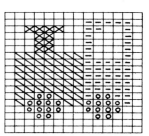

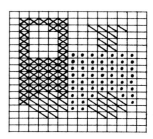

locomotive

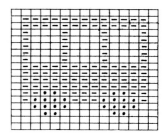

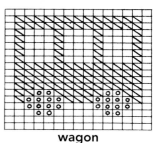

wagon

KEY TO CHART

☐	= ecru	⊟	= gold
◹	= light blue	·	= light pink
⊠	= gray blue	○	= rose

Baby booties

level
Intermediate

finished measurement
Length: 3-1/2 in. (9 cm)

materials
- Mayflower Cotton 8 - Sport weight yarn (approx. 186 yds per 50 g skein) 1 skein each color yellow, rose, and blue
- 2 buttons.
- Crochet hook U.S. size E/4 (Metric size 3.5).

gauge
13 sc and 15 rows = 4 in. (10 cm)

stitches
Chain (ch), slip st (sl), single crochet (sc), half double crochet (hdc)

Note: See pages 8–18 for detailed instructions on stitches and shapings.

Here are three sweet bootie styles designed to warm and comfort the little feet of the most discerning princess or prince.

Basic booties

Use these instructions for basic bootie.

sole

With crochet hook and double strand, ch 13. Round 1: 2 sc in 3rd ch from hook, 4 sc, 3 hdc, 1 dc, 3 dc in the foll ch, 2 dc in the last ch. Along the other side of the foundation ch, work as foll: 3 dc in the foll st, 1 dc, 1 hdc in each of the foll 3 sts, 4 sc, 2 sc in the last st. Sl st to join in the 2nd ch from the beg. Round 2: Ch 2, 2 sc in the foll st, 10 sc, 2 sc in each of the foll 6 sts, 10 sc, 2 sc in the last st. Sl st to join in the 2nd ch at the beg. Round 3: Ch 2, 2 sc in each of the foll 2 sts, 10 sc, 2 sc in each of the foll 3 sts, *1 sc in the foll st, 2 sc in the foll st*, rep * to * twice, 2 sc in each of the foll 3 sts, 10 sc, 2 sc in each of the foll 2 sts. Sl st to join in the 2nd ch at the beg. Continue in rounds, without sl st to join at end of round. Round 4: 1 sc in each sc, working through back loop only. Work foll rounds through both loops. Round 5: 16 sc, work foll 2 sc tog, *4 sc, 2 sc tog*, rep * to * twice, continue in sc. Round 6: Rep dec above previous ones. Round 7: Rep dec above previous dec, beg and end round with 2 sc tog. Round 8: Rep dec of the center front above previous ones. Sl st to join at center back. Fasten off.

Yellow booties

Foll above instructions to the 8th round, then work straps. After the 2nd dec = center front, ch 19. Sl st in the 7th ch from the hook = loop, sl st in each of the foll ch 5 for cross strap, ch 12, sl st in the 7th ch from the hook = 2nd loop, then sl st in each of the rem ch. Continue working the bootie. Sl st to join round. Sew end of loop to inside of bootie and sew button on opposite side. See photo.

Yellow & blue booties

Foll above instructions. Make the sole in yellow. Work the 4th to the 7th round in blue, work the 8th round in yellow. With yellow, make a chain 8 in. (20 cm) long. Sew chain 5 sc at center back, turn, make a ch 10 in. (25 cm) long. Fasten off.

Rose & blue booties

Foll above instructions for yellow/blue booties, but work the sole in rose, the 4th to the 7th row in blue and the 8th row and the straps in rose.

Sheep motif for baby

This nursery ensemble makes an enchanting shower gift for a mom-to-be who is soon to welcome a little sheep-counter.

level

Intermediate

finished measurement

Blanket: 23-1/2 x 28-3/4 in. (60 x 74 cm)

Bib: 6-3/4 x 6-1/2 in. (17.5 x 17 cm)

Bottle warmer: 10 in. (25 cm) high, bottom diameter 3-1/2 in. (9 cm)

Pincushion: 3-3/4 x 3-3/4 in. (9.5 x 9.5 cm)

materials

- Mayflower Cotton 8 - Sport weight cotton yarn (approx. 186 yds per 50 g skein)
- *Blanket:* 4 skeins color light green, 3 skeins light blue, and 2 skeins white
- *Bib:* 1 skein each color light green, light blue, white, and black
- *Bottle warmer:* 1 skein each color light green, light blue, white, and black
- *Pincushion:* 1 skein each color light green, light blue, white, and black

- Crochet hook U.S. size B/1 (Metric size 2.5)
- Afghan crochet hook size C/2 (Metric size 3) or size needed to obtain gauge

To save time, take time to check gauge!

gauge

19 sc and 23-1/2 rows = 4 in. (10 cm) for blanket

24 sts x 20 rows = 4 in. (10 cm) for bib, bottle warmer, and pincushion

stitches

Chain (ch), slip st (sl), single crochet (sc), half double crochet (hdc)

Tunisian st: Each row is worked back and forth, beg on a chain. Row 1: Yo, draw 1 loop through the 2nd ch from hook, yo, draw 1 loop through every foll loop. All loops stay on the hook. Row 2: Yo, draw through 1 loop, *yo, draw through 2 loops*, rep * to * so that 1 st rem on hook. Row 3: *Yo, insert hook through the vertical loop of the foll st and draw through 1 loop*, rep * to * so that all loops rem on the hook. Row 4: Yo, draw through 1 loop, *yo, draw through 2 loops*, rep * to * until 1 loop remains on hook. Always rep the 3rd and 4th rows.

Jacquard St: Foll chart in hdc. Beg each row with ch 2. When chang-ing colors, work the last loop of the last st with the color of the next st. Use small bobbins of yarn for each section of color.

Sheep stitch: Ch 5, work 1 sc in the 4th and 5th ch from the hook = 1 foot, ch 12, 1 sc in the 4th and the 5th ch from the hook = 2nd foot.

Row 1: Ch 3, 1 bobble in 1 foot (3 times in the same st: yo, draw through 1 loop until you have 7 loops, yo and draw through all loops), *ch 1, skip 1, 1 bobble*, work * to * 4 times, end with 1 dc = the 5th bobble counts as the 2nd foot. Row 2: Ch 3, 1 bobble between the first dc and the bob-

Blanket

With crochet hook and blue, ch 114 + ch 2 = first sc. Row 1: 1 sc in the 4th ch from hook = 112 sc. Work these 112 sc as foll: 10 rows in blue, *28 rows in green, 14 rows in blue*, rep * to * 3 times, 28 rows in green, 10 rows in blue = 174 rows. Work 1 round of sc in green around edges, working 2 sc in each corner st. Fasten off. Make 17 sheep and sew to top of blanket.

Bottle
warmer

For the top: with green, ch 64 and work in Tunisian st. Work 16 rows, then continue in blue until piece measures 8-1/4 in. (21 cm). Foll row: Work in eyelet st, *yo, draw 1 loop through 2 loops*, rep * to *, end with 1 loop on hook. Work until piece measures 10 in. (25 cm), end with 1 round of sl st as on bib.

Bottom: With green, ch 4 and sl st to join in a ring. End each row with 1 sl st. Ch 2 at the beg of round = first sc. Round 1: Ch 2, 7 sc in the ring = 8 sc. Round 2: 2 sc in each sc = 16 sc. Round 3: 2 sc in every 2nd sc = 24 sc. Rounds 4 to 8: Work 1 more sc between the incs of the previous row = 64 sc. Block pieces to indicated measurements. Embroider 3 sheep on the top part foll the chart. Embroider feet and ear in black. Sew back seam. Work 1 round of sc in green around top and lower edge. Fasten off. Work 1 round of sc in green around bottom and sew to top. Fasten off. Make a chain and thread through eyelet row.

ble, *ch 1, 1 bobble between the 2 bobbles*, work * to * 4 times, end with ch 1, 1 bobble between the last bobble and the dc, ch 1, 1 dc = 6 bobbles. Row 3: Work same as the 2nd row = 7 bobbles. Row 4: Ch 3, 1 bobble between the first and the 2nd bobble, *ch 1, 1 bobble between the foll 2 bobbles*, rep * to * 5 times, 1 dc = 6 bobbles. Now work 2 sc along the side seam on the 4th, 3rd and 2nd row for the head. Turn, ch 4, work 2 dc tog (worked in the 4th ch from the hook and the first sc), 1 dc in the foll sc, 1 hdc, 1 sc, ch 7, 1 sc in the 3rd ch from the hook, 1 hdc, 2 dc, 1 sc = ear, 1 sc in each of the last 2 sc. Row 5: Ch 1, 5 bobbles between the 6 bobbles with ch 1 between them, 1 dc. For the tail: 1 sc in the last dc and the edge dc of the 4th row, ch 7, 1 sc in the 7th ch from the hook, 3 sc. Break yarn leaving a long strand and thread through the last bobble and the edge dc of the 4th row and sew the last 3 sc tog. Using the same strand, sew sheep to crochet work. Embroider the gray eyes in daisy stitch. Sew tail and ear in place.

Note: See pages 8–18 for detailed instructions on stitches and shapings.

Bib

With green, ch 42. Work in tunisian st for 16 rows, then continue in blue for 14 rows. Work over the first 15 sts, then at neck edge, dec 1 st every 2nd row 3 times. On the 3rd row, dec 1 st at outside edge as well. End by slipping the last st through vertical post of underlying st. Work the 2nd half by slipping over center 12 sts, then work to correspond. Block piece to finished measurement. With green, work 1 row of sc around outside edges. Fasten off. With green, make a chain 8 in. (20 cm) long and join to neck edge. Make a 2nd tie. Cross-stitch sheep motifs on bib foll chart. Embroider the feet and ears in black.

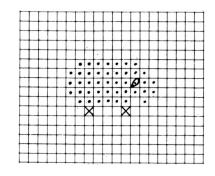

KEY TO CHART

⊠ = black

· = white

⊘ = black daisy stitch

Pincushion

Make 2 pieces. With green, ch 23 and work in Tunisian st as foll: work 9 rows in green and 10 rows in blue. End with 1 row of sl st as on bib. Fasten off. Embroider a sheep foll chart on one piece. Embroider feet and ear in black. Sew pieces tog, leaving an opening. Stuff and sew opening closed.

Duck ensemble

With its cheerful duck motif, this pincushion, sweater, and pair of booties make a charming gift set. Pink yarn can be substituted for the blue (girl and boy babies take to ducks the way ducks take to water!).

Duck pincushion

level

Intermediate

finished measurement

3 in. (8 cm); diameter of saucer: 4-1/2 in. (11 cm)

materials

- Mayflower Cotton 8 - Sport weight yarn (approx. 186 yds per 50 g skein) 1 skein each color light yellow, light orange, and light blue
- Fiberfill
- Steel crochet hook U.S. size 4 (Metric size 2) or size needed to obtain gauge

*To save time,
take time to check gauge!*

gauge

13 rows = 2 in. (5 cm)

stitches

Chain (ch), slip st (sl), single crochet (sc)

directions

duck

Worked in rounds. Mark the beg of each round. Do not join with a sl st unless otherwise indicated. Body: With light yellow, ch 4, sl st to join in ring. Round 1: 8 sc in ring. Round 2: 2 sc in every sc = 16 sc. Round 3: 2 sc in every 2nd sc = 24 sc. Round 4: 2 sc in every 3rd sc = 32 sc. Round 5: 32 sc. Round 6: 2 sc in every 6th sc = 37 sc. Rounds 7 to 14: 37 sc. Round 15: Sc, work every 6th and 7th sc tog. Round 16: 32 sc. Round 17: Sc, work every 3rd and 4th sc tog. Round 18: 24 sc. Round 19: Sc, work every 2nd and 3rd sc tog. Round 20: 16 sc, stuff body. Round 21: 2 sc tog, 6 sc, 2 sc tog, 6 sc. Round 22: 2 sc tog, 5 sc, 2 sc tog, 5 sc. Stuff the tail, flattening as you go. End with 1 row of sc through both thicknesses. Fasten off. Head: Work same as body through round 4. Rounds 5 to 11: 32 sc. Rounds 12 and 13: Sc, working every 2nd and 3rd sc tog. Stuff head. Work 2 sts tog around. Fasten off. Sew head to body. Beak: With light orange, ch 4, sl st to join in ring. Round 1: 8 sc in ring. Round 2: 2 sc in every sc = 16 sc. Round 3: 2 sc in every sc = 32 sc. Fasten off, leaving a thread. Fold beak in half and sew to head between the 9th and 10th rounds. Cross-st eyes in light blue. Skip 2 rows above the beak.

saucer

With light blue, ch 4, sl st to join in a ring. Round 1: 8 sc in ring. Round 2: 2 sc in each sc = 16 sc. Round 3: 2 sc in every 2nd sc = 24 sc. Round 4: 2 sc in every 3rd sc = 32 sc. Round 5: 2 sc in every 4th sc = 40 sc. Rounds 6 to 11: Work in this manner, inc 1 st above the previous incs = 1 more st between incs. Round 12: 88 sc. Round 13: Work in shrimp st (like sc, but worked left to right, instead of right to left). Sl st to join. Fasten off. Sew duck to center and flatten saucer.

Cardigan with ducks

level

Intermediate

size

Baby's size 3 (6, 9) months

finished measurement

Chest: 22 (23, 24) in.— 55 (57.5, 60.5) cm

Length: 10-1/4 (11, 11-1/2) in.— 26 (28, 29) cm

Sleeve seam with folded cuff: 7-1/4 (8, 8-1/2) in.—18.5 (20, 21.5) cm

materials

• Mayflower Cotton 8 - Sport weight cotton yarn (approx. 186 yds per 50 g skein) 3 (4, 4) skeins color blue, 1 skein each color white, yellow, and orange

• 3 buttons

• Crochet hook U.S. size C/2 (Metric size 3) or size needed to obtain gauge

• Knitting needles U.S. size 3 (Metric size 3)

To save time, take time to check gauge!

gauge

21 hdc and 14 rows = 4 in. (10 cm)

stitches

Chain (ch), slip st (sl), half double crochet (hdc)

Jacquard St: Foll chart in hdc. Beg each row with ch 2. When changing colors, work the last loop of the last st with the color of the next st. Use small bobbins of yarn for each section of color.

Striped pattern: Work in hdc as foll: Rows 1 and 2: *1 hdc with blue, 1 hdc with white, 1 hdc with blue*, rep * to *. Rows 3 to 8: With blue in hdc. Always rep rows 1 to 8.

1/1 ribbing: Row 1: *K1, p1*. Rep * to * across. Row 2 and all foll rows: Work sts as established in previous row.

Note: See pages 8–18 for detailed instructions on stitches and shapings.

directions

body

Worked entirely in hdc in striped pat and duck motif foll chart over every other stripe of blue. Work in 1 piece to armholes.

With crochet hook and blue, ch 111 (117, 123) + ch 2 = first hdc. Row 1: 1 hdc in the 4th ch from hook, 1 hdc in each of the foll ch = 111 (117, 123) hdc. Work 2 (4, 4) rows in blue. Continue in stripe pat. Work duck motif over blue rows as foll: 4 (7, 6) hdc in blue, *work from points 1 to 2 foll chart 1, 5 (5, 6) hdc with blue*, work * to * 8 times,

when piece measures 10-1/4 (11, 11-1/2) in.—26 (28, 29) cm. Work left front by rev shapings.

back

Leave 3 sts unworked at each edge for armhole. Work in striped pat as on front until same height as front, omitting neck shapings. Fasten off.

sleeves

With crochet hook and light blue, ch 33 (35, 37) + ch 2 = first hdc. Row 1: 1 hdc in the 4th ch from the hook, 1 hdc in each of the foll ch = 33 (35, 37) hdc. After 5 (6, 6) rows in blue, work in striped pat. At the same time, inc 1 st at each edge of every row 9 (10, 10) times = 51 (55, 57) dc. When sleeve measures 6-1/4 (7, 7-1/2) in.—16 (17.5, 19) cm, shape cap: Row 1: sl st over 5 (6, 6) sts, 6 sc, 29 (31, 33) hdc, 6 sc, sl st over 5 (6, 6) sts. Fasten off.

chart 1

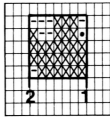

finishing

Block pieces to indicated measurements. Work 4 rows of sc along front edges in blue, alternately work 1 or 2 sc in each row. On the 3rd row make 3 buttonholes evenly spaced along top half of right front for girls and left front for boys by ch 2, skip 2 sc. On foll row, work 2 sc in ch 2. On last row, continue along neck edge, working 3 sc in each corner. Fasten off. With knitting needles and blue, pick up and knit 79 (81, 85) sts along neck edge, leaving front edges unworked. Work 2 in. (5 cm) in 1/1 ribbing, bind off loosely. With knitting needles and blue, pick up and knit 34 (36, 38) sts along each sleeve end and work 2 in. (5 cm) in 1/1 ribbing. Bind off loosely. Sew sleeves to armholes, sewing top of sleeve to underarm and sew sleeve seams, rev seam midway for cuffs. Fold cuffs to outside. Sew on buttons.

KEY TO CHART

⊠ = yellow

· = orange

⊟ = blue

then work from points 1 to 2 foll chart 1, end with 4 (7, 6) hdc with blue. Work 1 row of blue, continue in stripe pat for 20 (22, 22) rows = 5-1/2 (6, 6) in.—14 (15.5, 15.5) cm. Work separately for fronts and back.

right front

Work over the first 25 (27, 28) sts in stripe pat, working the first 6 rows in blue in duck motif as foll: 11 (18, 17) hdc with blue, work chart 1 once, work to end of row in blue. Continue until armhole measures 3-1/4 (3-1/2, 4) in.—8.5 (9, 10) cm. Shape Neck: At neck edge of every row, dec 4 (5, 5) sts once and dec 1 st 3 times. Fasten off

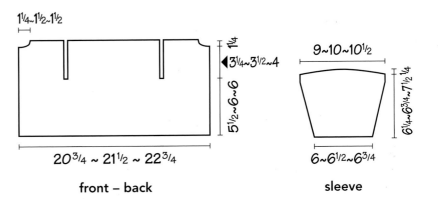

1¼~1½~1½

1¼

3¼~3½~4

5½~6~6

20¾ ~ 21½ ~ 22¾

front – back

9~10~10½

6¼~6¾~7½ 1¼

6~6½~6¾

sleeve

# Duck booties

stitches

Same as Cardigan

Work in blue for top of foot. Ch 9 + ch 2 = first hdc. Row 1: 1 hdc in the 4th ch from the hook, 1 hdc in each of the foll 7 ch = 9 hdc. Row 2: 1 hdc in blue, 6 hdc in yellow, 2 hdc in blue. Continue by foll chart 1. Fasten off after the 6th row. For the side pieces with blue, ch 12 (14), work 9 hdc in the right side of the last row of the top of the foot, ch 12 (14). Do not turn. Row 2: Ch 1 = 1 sc, 1 sc in the 3rd ch from the hook, 1 sc in each of the foll 10 (12) ch, continue along the side edges of the top of the foot, 11 sc, 9 sc along the foundation ch of the top of the foot, 11 sc along the side of the top of the foot, 1 sc in each of the foll 12 (14) ch = 55 (59) sc. Row 3: Alternately work 2 hdc with blue, 1 hdc with white. Break white strand and continue in blue. Row 4: 18 (19) hdc, 19 (21) sc, 18 (19) hdc. Row 5: Work 1 row of relief sc by working sc through the front post of the underlying st. On the right side of work, you will see a ridge. Fasten off.

sole

Work over the center 5 sts of the 5th row. Row 1: 5 hdc. Rows 2 and 3: 2 hdc in the first and last sts = 9 hdc. Rows 4 to 6 (7): 9 hdc. Rows 8, 10, 11, 12 (9, 11, 12, 13): hdc. Rows 7 (8), 9 (10) and 13 (14): Dec 1 st at each edge by working 2 hdc tog = 3 hdc. Fasten off. Work the border on the top edge as foll: with knitting needles and blue, pick up 33 (37) sts through the loops of the top of the foot plus 1 st extra = 34 (38) sts. Knit 1 row on right side of work. On the foll row: work 1 border st, *yo, k2 tog through back loops*, rep * to *, end with 1 border st = eyelet row. Work 2-1/2 in (6 cm) in 1/1 ribbing. Bind off loosely in ribbing.

finishing

Sew back seam, rev the seam for top half cuffs. Sew sole to sides as foll: sew the center st of the last row to the center back seam. Chain st a cord and thread through eyelet row, knotting at side.

chart 1

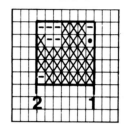

2   1

KEY TO CHART

⊠ = yellow

· = orange

☐ = white

Crocheted critters

Chickens

These soft, squeezable, and indestructible crocheted chickens (no detachable parts) are sure to delight a child.

level

Intermediate

finished measurement

Height 7 in. (18 cm)

materials

- Mayflower Cotton Helarsgarn - Worsted weight yarn (approx. 86 yds per 50 g skein) 1 skein each color white, yellow, red, rose, or blue
- Fiberfill
- Crochet hook U.S. size F/5 (Metric size 4) or size needed to obtain gauge

To save time, take time to check gauge!

gauge

9 sc = 2 in. (5 cm)

stitches

Chain (ch), slip st (sl), single crochet (sc)

Note: See pages 8–18 for detailed instructions on stitches and shapings.

directions

head and body

With white, ch 4, sl st to join in ring. Work in rounds and do not sl st to join unless specified. Round 1: 6 sc in ring, sl st to join. Mark beg of round. Round 2: 2 sc in each sc = 12 sc. Round 3: Sc, working 2 sc in every 2nd sc = 18 sc. Round 4: Sc, working 2 sc in every 3rd sc = 24 sc. Round 5: Sc, working 2 sc in every 4th sc = 30 sc. Round 6: Sc. Round 7: Sc, working 2 sc in every 4th sc = 37 sc. Rounds 8–10: Sc. Round 11: Sc, working 2 sc in every 5th sc = 44 sc. Rounds 12–14: Sc. Round 15: Sc, working every 4th and 5th st tog = 36 sc. Round 16: Sc. Round 17: Sc, working every 3rd and 4th sc tog = 27 sc. Round 18: Sc, working every 2nd and 3rd st tog = 18 sc. Round 19: With desired body color, work in sc, working 2 sc in every 3rd sc = 24 sc. Round 20: Sc. Round 21: Sc, working 2 sc in every 4th sc = 30 sc. Rounds 22–24: Sc. Round 25: Sc, working 2 sc in first 4 sc = 34 sc. Round 26: With white, sc, working 3 sc in 4th and 5th st = 38 sc. Round 27: Sc. Round 28: Work the 5th, 6th, 7th, and 8th sc tog, 1 sc in each sc = 35 sc. Round 29: Sc. Rounds 30 and 31: Sc, working every 3rd and 4th sc tog = 20 sc. Rounds 32 and 33: Sc, working every 2nd and 3rd sc tog = 9 sc. Stuff body, work 2 sc around until opening is closed. Fasten off.

wings

With white, ch 4, sl st to join in ring. Round 1: 6 sc in ring, do not sl st to join. Round 2: 2 sc in each sc = 12 sc. Round 3: Sc, working 2 sc in every 2nd sc = 18 sc. Rounds 4 and 5: Sc. Round 6: Sc, working every 2nd and 3rd sc tog = 12 sc. Rounds 7–9: Sc.

Round 10: Stuff the wing, fold flat and close opening by working 1 row of sc through both thicknesses. Fasten off. Make a 2nd wing.

bill

With yellow, ch 4, sl st to join in ring. Round 1: 5 sc in ring, do not sl st to join. Round 2: Sc, inc 2 sc around = 7 sc. Round 3: Sc, inc 3 sc around = 10 sc. Round 4: Sc, inc 4 sc around, end with 1 sl st. Break yarn.

legs

With yellow, ch 9 and sl st to join in ring. Rounds 1–3: Sc. Round 4: Work 2 sc in each of the first 4 sc, 1 sc in each sc = 13 sc. Round 5: Work 2 sc in the 3rd, 4th, 5th, and 6th sc, 1 sc in each sc, ending with 1 sl st. Break yarn. Make a 2nd leg.

feet

With yellow, ch 4 and sl st in ring. Round 1: 6 sc in ring. Round 2: Work 3 sc in the first and 2nd sc, continue by working 2 sc in each sc = 14 sc. Round 3: Work sc, working 2 sc in the 3rd, 4th, and 5th sc, sl st in the 6th sc. Break yarn. Make a 2nd foot.

finishing

Stuff the bill and sew between the 5th and 9th rounds from the neck and the head. Sew the wings to the sides with the rounded edge to front. Sew the feet to the legs, incs at front. Stuff the feet and sew between the first and 4th rounds from the bottom of the body. With blue, embroider eyes on the head 3 rounds high. With a strand of yarn, pull the eyes tog by connecting the eyes through the head. With white, make hair loops on top of head. See photo.

Duck & ducklings

This feathered family makes a very ducky gift (no feeding required!).

level
Intermediate

finished measurement
Duck: 8-1/2 in. (22 cm)
Ducklings: 4 in. (10 cm)

materials
- Mayflower Cotton 8 - Sport weight yarn (approx. 186 yds per 50 g skein) 1 skein each color dark brown, light brown, white, green, rust, and yellow
- Fiberfill
- 4 sets of small brown eyes and 1 set of large brown eyes
- Crochet hook U.S. size C/2 (Metric size 2.5) or size needed to obtain gauge

To save time, take time to check gauge!

gauge

25 sc and 26 rows = 4 in. (10 cm)

stitches

Chain (ch), slip st (sl), single crochet (sc)

Note: See pages 8–18 for detailed instructions on stitches and shapings.

directions

head

With crochet hook and green, ch 4 + ch 1 = first st. Sl st to join in ring. Work in rounds of sc, but do not sl st to join unless indicated. Mark beg of round. Round 1: 6 sc in ring, sl st to join. Round 2: 2 sc in each sc = 12 sc. Round 3: Sc, working 2 sc in every 2nd sc = 18 sc. Round 4: Sc, working 2 sc in every 3rd sc = 24 sc. Round 5: Sc, working 2 sc in every 4th sc = 30 sc. Round 6: Sc, working 2 sc in every 5th sc = 36 sc. Round 7: Sc. Round 8: Sc, working 2 sc in every 6th sc = 42 sc. Rounds 8 and 9: Sc. Round 10: Sc, working 2 sc in every 7th sc = 48 sc. Rounds 10–13: Sc. Round 14: Sc, working 3 sc in the first, 2nd, and 19th and 20th sc (cheeks), work 1 sc in rem sc = 56 sc. Rounds 15–20: Sc. Round 21: Sc, working every 6th and 7th sc tog. Rounds 22–23: Sc. Round 24: Sc, work every 5th and 6th sc tog = 40 sc. Round 25: Sc, work every 4th and 5th sc tog = 32 sc. Rounds 26–29: Sc. Round 30: 2 sc in every 8th sc = 36 sc. Round 32: 2 sc in every 9th sc = 40 sc. Round 33: Sc. Round 34: With white for neck: 2 sc in every 10th sc = 44 sc. Round 36: 2 sc in every 11th sc = 48 sc. Fasten off.

body

With dark brown, work same as first 6 rounds of head = 36 sc. Round 7: 2 sc in every 6th sc = 42 sc. Round 8: 2 sc in every 7th sc = 48 sc. Round 9: Sc. Round 10: 2 sc in every 8th sc = 54 sc. Round 11: 2 sc in every 9th sc. Round 12: 2 sc in every 10th sc = 66 sc. Round 13: 2 sc in every 11th sc = 72 sc. Round 14: 2 sc in every 12th sc = 78 sc. Round 15: Sc. Round 16: 2 sc in every 13th sc = 84 sc. Rounds 17–29: Sc. Round 30: Sc in white. Rounds 31–43: Sc. Round 44: Sc, working every 6th and 7th sc tog = 72 sc. Rounds 45–47: Sc. Round 48: Sc, working every 5th and 6th sc tog = 60 sc. Rounds 49–51: Sc. Round 52: Sc, working every 4th and 5th sc tog. Rounds 53–56: Sc. Round 57: Sc, working every 3rd and 4th sc tog = 36 sc. Rounds 58–63: Sc. Round 64: Sc, work every 2nd and 3rd sc tog. Round 65: Sc. Round 66: 3 sc tog twice, 6 sc, work 3 sc tog twice, 6 sc = 16 sc (the dec are at each side of tail). Rounds 67–69: Sc. Round 70: Sc. Continue in dark brown and stuff body and tail. Rounds 71–75: Sc. Round 76: Work every 2nd and 3rd sc tog = 11 sc. Work 2 sc tog around until opening is closed. Fasten off.

wings

With white, work first 4 rounds as on head = 24 sc. Round 5: Sc. Round 6: 2 sc in every 4th sc = 30 sc. Round 7: Sc. Round 8: 2 sc in every 5th sc = 36 sc. Round 9: 2 sc in every 6th sc = 42 sc. Round 10: Sc. Round 11: 2 sc in every 7th sc = 48 sc. Round 12: Sc. Round 13: 2 sc in every 8th sc = 54 sc. Round 14: 2 sc in every 9th sc = 60 sc. Rounds 15–20: Sc. Round 21: Sc, work every 5th and 6th sc tog = 50 sc. Rounds 22 and 23: Sc. Round 24: Sc, work every 4th and 5th sc tog = 40 sc. Rounds 25 and 26: Sc. Round 27: Sc, work every 3rd and 4th sc tog = 30 sc. Rounds 28–31: Sc. Round 32: Sc, work every 2nd and 3rd sc tog = 20 sc. Rounds 33–36: Sc. Round 37: Sc, work 2 sc tog around = 10 sc. Rounds 38–40: Sc. Round 41: Sc, work 2 sc tog around, continuing until opening is closed. Fasten off. Make a 2nd wing.

top beak

With rust, working same as first 3 rounds as head = 18 sc. Round 4: Sc. Round 5: 2 sc in every 6th sc = 21 sc. Rounds 6–10: Sc. Round 11: 2 sc in every 3rd sc = 28 sc. Round 12: 2 sc in every 4th sc = 35 sc. Stuff top beak lightly and fold double, and work 1 row of sc through both thicknesses. Fasten off.

lower beak

With rust, work first 2 rounds same as head = 12 sc. Round 3: 2 sc in every 4th sc = 15 sc. Rounds 4–7: Sc. Round 8: 2 sc in every 5th sc = 18 sc. Round 9: Sc. Round 10: 2 sc in every 6th sc = 21 sc. Round 11: Stuff lower beak and fold double and work 1 row of sc through both thicknesses. Fasten off.

feathers

Make 4 dark brown, 2 light brown and 3 white feathers. Work first 2 rounds same as head = 12 sc. Rounds 3–11: 12 sc. Break yarn, leaving an end 8 in. (20 cm) long.

finishing

Stuff head and sew to opening of body between the 10th and 28th rounds of body. The incs for the cheeks come to the front. Sew on the top beak between the 14th and 19th rounds of head. See photo. The center of the top beak is on the 14th round and the side seams are on the 19th round.

With dark brown, embroider nostrils in outline stitch over the 9th and 10th rounds, spaced 3 sc apart on the 9th round and 5 sc on the 10th round. Sew the lower beak between the 21st and 23rd rounds with the center of the lower beak on the 23rd round and the sides on the 21st round. Sew eyes on the 12th round of the head 18 sc apart. Insert the needle through both sides of the head and attach 1 eye, then pull through head and attach 2nd eye. Flatten the wings and sew to each side of the body. Beg with the 4th round of the wing on the 17th round on the body. The top edge of the wing comes 7 sc under the neck. Leave the last 9 rounds of feathers loose. Sew on feather with the hanging thread on the top edge. Sew white feather in the center of the 25th round of the body. Sew 1 light brown feather along 3 sc and on the 29th round. Sew a dark brown feather slanted between the 25th to the 29th rounds with 4 sc between them, 4 sc above the white feather with 1 sc above the light brown feather. Sew white feather in the center of the tail on the 61st round. Sew 2 dark brown feathers slanted between the 61st and 64th rounds with 1 sc between them on the 64th round.

$\mathcal{D}$ucklings

head

With light brown, dark brown, or yellow, ch 4 and sl st to join in ring. Round 1: 6 sc in ring. Round 2: 2 sc in every sc = 12 sc. Round 3: 2 sc in every 2nd sc = 18 sc. Round 4: Sc. Round 5: 2 sc in every 3rd sc = 24 sc. Round 6: 2 sc in every 4th sc = 30 sc. Round 7: 2 sc in every 5th sc = 36 sc. Rounds 8–13: Sc. Round 14:

Sc, work every 5th and 6th sc tog = 30 sc. Round 15: Sc, work every 4th and 5th sc tog = 24 sc. Round 16: Sc, work every 3rd and 4th sc tog = 18 sc. Round 17: 18 sc. Fasten off.

body

With light brown, dark brown, or yellow, work the first 3 rounds of head = 18 sc. Round 4: 2 sc in every 3rd sc = 24 sc. Round 5: Sc. Round 6: 2 sc in every 4th sc = 30 sc. Round 7: 2 sc in every 5th sc = 36 sc. Round 8: 2 sc in every 6th sc = 42 sc. Rounds 9–14: Sc. Round 15: Work every 6th and 7th sc tog = 36 sc. Rounds 16–19 sc. Round 20: Sc, work every 5th and 6th sc tog = 30 sc. Round 21: Sc. Round 22: Work 2 sc tog 5 times - underside of body, continue in sc - 25 sc. Round 23: Sc. Round 24: 2 sc tog 3 times, continue in sc = 22 sc. Stuff body. Round 25: Sc. Stuff. Round 26: Sc, working every 2nd and 3rd sc tog = 15 sc. Round 27: Sc, working every 2nd and 3rd sc tog = 10 sc. Round 28: Fold tail double and sew to the 22nd and 24th rounds on the underside. Work 2 sc tog around until opening is closed. Fasten off.

Make a wing in light brown, dark brown, or yellow foll the first 3 rounds of head = 18 sc. Rounds 4–10: Sc. Round 11: Stuff feather lightly and work every 2nd and 3rd sc tog = 12 sc. Round 12: Sc. Round 13: Work 2 sc tog until opening is closed. Make a 2nd wing.

Make the beak in rust, working same as first 2 rounds of head = 12 sc. Rounds 3–4: Sc. Round 5: 2 sc in every 4th sc = 15 sc. Break yarn, leaving end 8 in. (20 cm) long.

finishing

Stuff head and sew to body between the 6th and the 13th rounds. Sew a wing to each side of body. Beg with the 3rd round of wing on the 8th round of the body. See photo. Stuff the beak and sew to head between the 10th and 16th rounds. Sew eyes to the 8th round with 8 sc between them, same as duck.

Make 1 light brown, 1 dark brown, and 2 yellow ducklings. Over the head, body, and wings, make yellow dots, embroidering 2 satin sts over 1 sc.

Mohair kittens

A purrrr-fect present for that child or young-at-heart adult who can appreciate cuddling up to a pair of kittens as soft as the real thing.

level

Intermediate

finished measurement

Height: 6 in. (15 cm)

Length: 7-1/2 in. (19 cm)

materials

- Mohair yarn, 1 skein each color pink and white
- 2 pink buttons
- Fiberfill
- Ribbon
- Dark pink tapestry wool
- A small hook
- Crochet hook U.S. size C/2 (Metric size 3) or size needed to obtain gauge

gauge

11 sc and 10 rows = 4 in. (10 cm)

stitches

Chain (ch), slip st (sl), single
crochet (sc)

Note: See pages 8–18
for detailed instructions
on stitches and shapings.

White kitten

With crochet hook and white ch
4, sl st to join in ring. Now work
in rounds, but do not sl st to join
at end of round unless specified.
Round 1: 6 sc in ring, sl st to join.
Round 2: Sc, working 2 sc in each
st = 12 sc. Round 3: Sc, working
2 sc in every 2nd st = 18 sc.
Rounds 4 and 5: Sc, working 2 sc
in every 4th st = 28 sc. Round 6:
Sc, working 2 sc in every 5th st =
33 sc. Round 7: Sc. Round 8: Sc,
working 2 sc in every 5th st = 39
sc. Round 9: Sc. Round 10: Sc,
working 2 sc in every 6th st = 45
sc. Rounds 11 - 14: Sc. Round 15:
Sc, working 2 sc in every 4th st =
56 sc. Rounds 16 - 19: Sc. Round
20: Work 2 sc tog 4 times, 10 sc,
2 sc worked tog 4 times (these
decs will be the cheeks), now
work every 3rd and 4th sc tog =
41 sc. Round 21: Sc. Round 22:
Sc, work every 3rd and 4th sc tog
= 31 sc. Round 23: Sc and stuff
head. Round 24: Sc and work
every 3rd and 4th sc tog = 24 sc.
Round 24: Sc and work every 2nd
and 3rd sc tog = 16 sc. Stuff head
and work 2 sc tog around on next
rounds until opening is closed.

body

With white, ch 4 and sl st to join in ring = tail end of body. Round 1: Work 6 sc in ring. Round 2: Sc, work 2 sc in each sc = 12 sc. Round 3: Sc, work 2 sc in every 2nd sc = 18 sc. Rounds 4–6: Sc, working 2 sc in every 4th sc = 35 sc. Rounds 7 and 8: Sc. Round 9: Work 16 sc = back, inc 5 sc across rem sc = 40 sc. Rounds 10–15: Sc. Round 16: Work 16 sc for back, work every 3rd and 4th sc tog across rem sc = 34 sc. Round 17: Sc. Round 18: Sc, work 3 sc in the 4th, 7th, 10th, and 13th sc of the back = 42 sc. Rounds 19–21: Sc. Round 22: Sc, work every 4th and 5th sc tog = 34 sc. Round 23: Sc, work every 3rd and 4th sc tog = 26 sc. Stuff body. Round 24: Sc, work every 2nd and 3rd sc tog = 18 sc. Work 2 sc tog around until the opening is closed. Fasten off.

front feet

With pink, ch 4 and sl st to join in ring. Round 1: Work 6 sc in ring. Round 2: Sc, work 2 sc in every sc = 12 sc. Round 3: Continue in white, sc, work 2 sc in every 3rd sc = 15 sc. Rounds 4–7: Sc. Round 8: 5 sc, turn, skip 1 sc, 4 sc and sl 1. Fasten off. Make a 2nd foot.

back feet

Work same as front feet to the 5th round. Round 6: Turn and work 8 sc, turn, skip the first sc, 6 sc and sl 1. Fasten off. Make a 2nd foot.

tail

With white, ch 4 and sl st to join in ring. Round 1: 6 sc in ring. Round 2: Work 2 sc in every sc = 12 sc. Rounds 3–14: Sc. Fasten off.

ears

Make 2 ears in white, 2 ears in pink. Ch 19 and work in sc. Ch 1 = first sc. Rows 1 and 2: 19 sc. Rows 3 and 4: Sc, work the center 3 sc tog = 15 sc. Row 5: Insert hook through the top loop of the sc sts. Fasten off.

nose

With pink, ch 3 and sl st to join in ring. Round 1: 6 sc in ring. Round 2: Sc and work 4 sc in the first and 4th sc = 12 sc. Round 3: Sc. Round 4: Sc, work 2 sc in every 3rd sc = 16 sc. Round 5: Sc, work 2 sc in every 3rd sc = 21 sc. Fasten off.

Pink kitten

Work head, tail, nose, and ears same as white kitten, but use pink for white and white for pink.

body

Work same as white kitten to the 6th round. Rounds 7–22: 35 sc. Round 23: sc, work every 3rd and 4th sc tog = 27 sc. Stuff body. Round 24: Sc, work every 2nd and 3rd sc tog = 18 sc. Work 2 sc tog around until opening is closed. Fasten off.

front feet

Work same as white kitten to the 7th round. Work 2 rounds in sc. Fasten off.

back feet

Work same as front feet to 7th round. Round 8: Sc, work 2 sc in the first, 2nd, and 3rd sc, and work the 8th and 9th sts, the 10th and 11th sts, the 12th and 13th sts tog = 16 sc. Round 9: Sc, work 2 sc in the 2nd, 4th, and 6th sc for the front edge and work 2 sc tog above the previous decs. Work 1 row over the 16 sc and fasten off.

finishing

Stuff kittens and tails. White kitten: Sew the front feet to the body between the 6th and 12th rounds from the neck, with 2 sc between them. Sew back feet, between the 5th and 14th rounds from the tail end. Sew head to body, with the underside of chin sewn to body. Stuff nose and sew between cheeks (round 20). Sew 1 pink and 1 white piece of ear tog and work 1 round of sc in white along edge. Sew on ears 3/4 in. (2 cm) apart. Embroider nose with dark pink in satin st over 3 sc. See photo. Sew on buttons for eyes, using a double strand of yarn pulled through head. Tie ribbon around neck. Sew on tail. Pink Kitten: Sew back feet between the 5th and 13th rounds with 2 sc between them. Sew front feet between the 8th and 9th rounds from the top. Sew on tail. Sew head to body as on white kitten. Complete as white kitten.

Teddy bear

This picture says it all.
All you have to do
is make the bear!

level
Intermediate

finished measurement
Length: 11 in. (28 cm)

materials
- Worsted weight yarn (approx. 93 yds per 50 g skein) 2 skeins color beige, 1 skein each color yellow and red
- Plastic nose and 2 eyes
- 2 buttons
- Fiberfill
- Crochet hook U.S. size C/2 (Metric size 3) or size needed to obtain gauge

To save time, take time to check gauge!

gauge
16 sc and 18 rows = 4 in. (10 cm)

stitches
Chain (ch), slip st (sl), single crochet (sc)

Note: See pages 8–18 for detailed instructions on stitches and shapings.

directions
Work in sc in rounds. Do not join with a sl st at end of round unless otherwise indicated. Mark beg of round. Work through both loops of st of previous round.

head
With beige, ch 4 and sl st in a ring. Round 1: Work 6 sc in a ring. Round 2: 2 sc in every sc = 12 sc. Round 3: Sc, work in 2 sc in every 3rd sc = 16 sc. Rounds 4 and 5: Sc, work 2 sc in every 3rd sc = 28 sc. Round 6: Sc. Round 7: Sc, work 2 sc in every 5th sc = 33 sc. Rounds 8 and 9: Sc. Round 10: 1 sc in each of the first and last 4 sc of the previous round and space 12 incs over the rem 25 sc = 45 sc. Round 11: 1 sc in each of the first and last 4 sc and inc 1 sc in every 2nd sc of the rem 37 sc = 18 inc. Rounds 12–22: 63 sc. Attach the plastic nose on the right side of the foundation ring. Round 23: 1 sc in each of the first 6 sc, work 2 sc tog 5 times, 31 sc, work 2 sc tog 5 times, 1 sc in each of the last 6 sc = 53 sc. Rounds 24–26: Sc. Round 27: Sc, work every 3rd and 4th sc tog = 40 sc. Round 28: Sc. Round 29: Sc, work every 2nd and 3rd sc tog = 27 sc. Stuff head and continue. Round 30: Work 2nd and 3rd sc tog = 18 sc. Then sc around. Fasten off.

ears
With beige, ch 4 and sl st to join in ring. Round 1: 6 sc in ring. Round 2: 2 sc in each sc = 12 sc. Round 3: Sc, work 2 sc in every 3rd sc = 16 sc. Round 4: Sc, work 2 sc in every 3rd sc = 21 sc. Round 5: Sc. Round 6: Sc, work 2 sc in every 3rd sc = 28 sc. Round 7: Work 2 sc in every 3rd sc = 37 sc. Round 8: Sc. Round 9: Sc, work every 3rd and 4th sc tog = 28 sc. Round 10: Sc. Round 11: Sc, work every 3rd and 4th sc tog = 21 sc. Fasten off. Fold ear in half and sew opening closed. Make a 2nd ear.

body
With yellow, ch 4 and sl st to join in a ring. Round 1: 6 sc in a ring. Round 2: 2 sc in every sc = 12 sc. Round 3: Sc, work 2 sc in every 2nd sc = 18 sc. Round 4: Sc, work 2 sc in every 3rd sc = 24 sc. Round 5: Sc, work 2 sc in every 3rd sc = 32 sc. Round 6: Sc, 2 sc in every 4th sc = 40 sc. Round 7: Sc. Round 8: Sc, work 2 sc in every 4th sc = 50 sc. Rounds 9–17: Sc. Round 18: Sc, work every 3rd and 4th sc tog = 38 sc. Rounds 19–24: Sc. Round 25: Sc, work every 3rd and 4th sc tog = 29 sc. Round 26: Sc and fasten off = neck edge.

legs
With beige, ch 4 and sl st to join in ring. Round 1: Work 6 sc in a ring. Round 2: 2 sc in every sc = 12 sc. Round 3: 4 sc in the first sc, 1 sc in the foll sc, 4 sc in the foll sc = front, complete in sc = 18 sc. Round 4: Sc, work 2 sc in every 4th sc = 22 sc. Round 5: Sc, work 2 sc in every 4th sc = 27 sc. Rounds 6 and 7: Sc. Round 8: Work 2 sc tog over the first 10 sc = front, complete in sc = 22 sc. Round 9: Work 2 sc tog 3 times, 16 sc = 19 sc. Rounds 10–13: Sc. Round 14: 2 sc in each of the first 4 sc, 15 sc = 23 sc. Rounds 15 and 16: Sc. Fasten off. Work the 2nd leg in the same manner.

arms
With beige, ch 4 and sl st to join. Round 1: Work 6 sc in ring. Round 2: 2 sc in every sc = 12 sc. Rounds 3–6: Sc, work 2 sc in every 4th sc = 29 sc. Rounds 7 and 8: Sc. Round 9: Sc, work every 3rd and 4th sc tog = 22 sc. Round 10: Sc, work every 3rd and 4th sc tog = 17 sc. Work 8 more rounds in sc, then fasten off. Make a 2nd arm.

tail
With beige, ch 4 and sl st to join in ring. Round 1: Work 6 sc in ring. Round 2: 2 sc in every sc = 12 sc. Round 3: 2 sc in every 4th sc = 15 sc. Rounds 4 and 5: Sc, work 2 sc in every 4th sc = 23 sc. Round 6: Sc. Round 7: Work every 2nd and 3rd sc tog = 16 sc. Fasten off.

pant legs

With yellow, ch 38 and sl st to join in ring. Round 1: 1 sc in every ch st = 38 sc. Rounds 2–5: Sc. Fasten off.

sleeves

With yellow, ch 28 and sl st to join in ring. Round 1: 1 sc in every ch st = 28 sc. Rounds 2 and 3: Sc. Round 4: *2 sc tog, 1 sc*, rep * to *, end with 2 sc tog = 18 sc. Pull the sleeve over 1 arm and join the top rounds of sleeves and arms. Fasten off.

back pockets

With red, ch 8. Row 1: Sc, work the first sc in the 2nd ch from the hook. Work 5 rows in sc, ch 1 to turn at beg of each row. Fasten off. Make a 2nd pocket.

front pocket

With red, ch 14 and work 7 rows in sc same as back pocket. Fasten off.

---

finishing

Stuff arms, legs, and body. With double strand, gather the top row of body and sew head between the 9th and the 18th row. Sew the ears to the head with 10 sc between them. See photo. Sew on the eyes with 17 sc between them and 12 rows above the nose. Sew on 1 eye, thread yarn through the head and come up at position of 2nd eye and pull into head. 8 rows under the eyes, embroider the mouth in satin st. Stuff the tail and sew to body between the 9th and 12th row from the beg. Sew arms and legs to body. Roll the pants legs over the body and sew to yellow body. Sew small pockets to back near the tail and sew large pocket on front. With double strand of red, embroider line in red. See photo. Sew on buttons. Roll up pants legs and sleeves.

INDEX